Prais

THE MAG

"This book delivers! Howard's simple and relatable story shares a powerful message that should be read by everyone. THE MAGIC CUP reminds us to give more than we take to find your true path to happiness."

—WENDY COLLIE, CEO, New Seasons Market, and former SVP, Starbucks Corporation

"THE MAGIC CUP beautifully illustrates that there's nothing more powerful than TEAM when passion, a focus on a purpose beyond profits, and sheer will to ensure everyone around you thrives is at its center."

—KIP TINDELL, Chairman and CEO, The Container Store

"When people join your purpose, not just your company, you get engagement. Engagement is a super power that makes problems disappear, aligns teams, and creates loyal consumers. It gives our work meaning. No one understands this better than Howard Behar." —CHRISTINE DAY, CEO, Luvo, Inc.

THE MAGIC CUP's parable of modern business life could not be timelier. Howard Behar, a business hero if there ever was one, reminds us of the power of human values and purpose and the possibility for creating a different type of company—and the many rewards from doing so."

—JEFFREY PFEFFER, author of *Leadership BS: Fixing Workplaces and Careers One Truth at a Time*

The MAGIC CUP

A Business Parable About a Leader, a Team,
and the Power of Putting People
and Values First

Howard Behar

With Lorie Ann Grover and Dia Calhoun
Foreword by Jeff Brotman,
Co-founder and Chairman of Costco

CENTER STREET

New York   Boston   Nashville

Center Street
Hachette Book Group
1290 Avenue of the Americas, New York, NY 10104
centerstreet.com
twitter.com/centerstreet

Originally published in hardcover in 2016 by Center Street.
First trade paperback edition: March 2017

Center Street is a division of Hachette Book Group, Inc. The Center Street name and logo are trademarks of Hachette Book Group, Inc.

The publisher is not responsible for websites (or their content) that are not owned by the publisher.

The Hachette Speakers Bureau provides a wide range of authors for speaking events. To find out more, go to www.HachetteSpeakersBureau.com or call (866) 376-6591.

LCCN: 2015043093
ISBN: 978-1-4555-3898-0 (trade pbk.)

Printed in the United States of America

LSC-C

10 9 8 7 6 5 4 3 2 1

For Lynn
The love of my life

Contents

A Note to Readers

Welcome to the story of the Magic Cup. Think of it as a business adventure tale or a modern fable. The events it relates may be make-believe but the story it conveys is real. I've lived it.

Long after the directives, the memos, the leadership lessons, and the PowerPoints are over, it's the stories and experiences that stick with us and guide us. Our big plans and small wins, our trials and tribulations, our desperation and elation, our perseverance and moments of personal greed, our near misses and rare triumphs teach us one truth: *Success comes when we believe in something that is bigger than ourselves.*

There's magic when a group of people is bound together with common purpose. It's the chemistry of real people, doing the right things, with the right set of values. The journey to discover that magic—to create it with the people on our team—is what this tale is all about.

Enjoy the adventure.

Foreword

You're about to embark on a wonderful journey in the story of *The Magic Cup* and the wisdom of Howard Behar wrapped in its pages.

Howard Behar represents a special kind of person, friend, and leader. Since he first swept the floors of his father's grocery store, he was learning the lessons that would shape the culture of every company he helped grow and lead, most remarkably during his twenty years working to build the Starbucks organization and championing its people-centered principles around the world.

I've known Howard from our school days when we both were growing up, as kids in Seattle. It's clear there was something special in the air we were raised in. Seattle was really a small town then and we were part of a loose-knit tribe where everyone looked out for each other, and we didn't know or care how much money you had or what your father or mother did for a living. Growing up in this culture with strong values was both of our stories. It was the same for the Nordstrom kids and Bill Gates. Values drove the city.

It was an accident of birth that our lives got started in a city of hard-working, caring immigrants that came from all over the world. Looking back, I believe a blending of those cultures gave rise to a subdued, basic, un-fancy personality type that rewarded hard work, creating things, entrepreneurialism, and an appreciation for community.

When I co-founded Costco with Jim Sinegal, we shared the

desire to create a culture in keeping with the Seattle inclusiveness and fairness I grew up with. We were guided by our ethics and created a family atmosphere in which our employees could thrive and succeed. And we were driven by trust and quality in everything we did, from our products and pricing for our customers to our commitment to our employees.

That's where Howard Behar comes in. A few years into our enormous growth at Costco, Howard Schultz, the founder of the Starbucks we know today, asked me if I could help him put together a management structure and team shortly after he and a group of investors bought the company. He had the idea of transforming a simple coffee bean company into an actual coffee shop company, Italian-inspired cafés where people could drink coffee and spend time together.

I knew Howard Behar was the right person to help Starbucks grow and thrive as a place for people. He had the right heart, drive, and caring. He was in the business of positive thought and positive action. He was a person with great vision and the sense of the potential in people. Howard makes the people around him feel safe. It didn't surprise me when Howard became known as the soul of Starbucks for the twenty years he was there, as it grew into a worldwide coffee company.

Yet not all of us are surrounded by the type of family I had, the grocery store Howard grew up in, or the straightforward, honest, and open culture of Seattle itself. Without a foundation we flounder. Without a moral compass we lack in moral decision-making. We can know the right thing to do, but it can seem too hard to actually do.

The gift of the book you have in your hands, *The Magic Cup*, is in helping every one of us think about and develop our own personal foundation. It tells a great story with a great message we can all take to heart: We need to continually reaffirm our core values and surround ourselves with people who share those same values. Values are not a declaration of policy. Our values come into being when we live them and build on them, when they are visible.

That's what the characters in *The Magic Cup* are on a quest to do. While the story of Steadfast, the new CEO at Verity Glassworks, is fiction, the underlying truth is something that many companies and leaders have gone through.

Everyone in the workplace today, including frontline employees, aspiring leaders, and executive leadership, will benefit from the lessons of Steadfast, his mentor, and his new colleagues. Using the power of story, Behar helps us get away from a relentless desire for fast profit and an accompanying lack of focus on building something of substance that will last. We spend way too much time on short-term, transactional goals and not nearly enough time on the people who bring our organizations to life.

The drumbeat of overnight success, money, and fame is all around us with an impact that reaches from Wall Street to pop culture, to the news and our business schools. Howard Behar provides us with something more substantial—an antidote, an inoculation, to connect us to our deeper principles and the foundation that matters.

Companies like Costco, Starbucks, and Nordstrom have proven over and over again that when the rewards—both tangible and intangible in terms of respect and caring—are shared with employees, everyone benefits, including shareholders. No matter what the size of your organization or its financial results, all of us can build success with the people around us when we have the foundations and lessons you'll discover in the journey of *The Magic Cup*.

I am so fortunate to have had Howard Behar's friendship and wisdom for so many decades and I am happy you'll be able to have a piece of it for yourself with this charming book. Its substantial and deep message is one we all need to hear and heed.

Jeff Brotman

One evening an old Cherokee grandfather told his grandson about a battle that goes on inside all people.

He said, "My son, the battle is between two 'wolves' inside us all. One is Evil. It is anger, envy, jealousy, sorrow, regret, greed, arrogance, self-pity, guilt, resentment, inferiority, lies, false pride, superiority, and ego.

"The other is Good. It is joy, peace, love, hope, serenity, humility, kindness, benevolence, empathy, generosity, truth, compassion and faith."

The grandson thought about it for a minute and then asked his grandfather, "Which wolf wins?"

The Grandfather simply replied...

"The one you feed."

—Author Unknown

PROLOGUE

Dear Steadfast,

To celebrate your new role as CEO of Verity Glassworks—a position in which I know you will meet every challenge and excel—I give you this glass cup to guide your journey and inspire your leadership. Always keep your cup full and your life will overflow with joy.

Warmly,
Nora

CHAPTER 1

Ready to Lead

> If you do your job well enough and if you are committed enough to your task, good things can happen.
>
> —Steadfast

The sun came out from behind the clouds as Vince Steadfast stepped onto the street from the underground parking garage. He didn't want to allow himself to get too excited about where he was going. After all, it would be unseemly for someone in his position to appear too enthusiastic. But the simple fact was, his heart was soaring. He'd always taken great pride in the way his career had continued its gradual progression. His wife called him "a glacier," referring to his slow but steady approach, and she meant it as a compliment. But he was about to make a giant leap.

The city of Harken was gleaming, as though nature had bequeathed an extra sheen for this first day of Steadfast's greatest adventure. Harken had been one of the world's most dynamic cities for more than half a century thanks to its combination of culture, innovation, opportunity, and physical beauty. Over the past decade Harken had become something of an inspiration for cities everywhere as it continued to prosper, even in the face of global economic worries. Steadfast was proud of his city and glad to play even the tiniest part in its growing prominence.

The most distinctive landmark on the Harken skyline was the soaring Verity Tower, a block to the left of where Steadfast was currently standing. The sun glinted off the signature dome causing the crystal cupola to sparkle like a diamond that could be seen from every corner of the city. Its reputation around the world was on par with such iconic peers as the Empire State Building in New York, the Lloyd's building in London and the Burj Khalifa in Dubai, but in Steadfast's opinion, it was far more beautiful than any of them, architectural majesty in its grandest form.

There's magic there, Steadfast thought, surprising himself. Magic had always seemed like something fanciful to him, the stuff of children's stories and street illusionists. It had no place in his life, especially his business life. If "magic" ever happened in business, it was the result of hard work and dedication. Steadfast believed if you did your job well enough and if you were committed enough to your task, good things would happen.

And good things had indeed happened for Steadfast. Today was his first day as CEO of Verity Glassworks, one of the finest old companies in the city, one that predated most of the city proper but continued to define it. Verity had been founded more than a century earlier as a manufacturer of artisan pieces, gorgeously intricate glass creations. The artisan part of the business had died away a few decades ago due to market forces and a shaky international economy. However, Verity kept its bottom line strong by transitioning to become one of the most significant bottle manufacturers in the country. Verity products sat in refrigerators and pantries these days rather than on living room mantels; some people mourned this fact, even going so far as to say that Verity was just another corporation now. But Steadfast understood. Art was a luxury; commerce was a necessity.

For the past five years, Steadfast had been vice president of operations at Noblecorp, a holding company for a diverse range of consumer goods enterprises. He was happy there, and well compensated, but his access to the upper echelons was blocked by a long-established group of effective executives, headed by CEO Nora Northstar. Steadfast knew that at some point he was going to have to make a move if he wanted to be anything more than "the glacier." This thought had come to mind when he heard that Verity's latest CEO had abruptly resigned. He was still contemplating whether he should go after the job when Nora called him into her office.

"I assume you've heard that Kacen is gone from Verity."

"I've heard. What is that, three in four years?"

Nora shook her head slowly. "It's sad, really, especially when you think about how people used to study Verity's leaders in business schools. Now..."

She trailed off, and Steadfast wasn't sure if he was supposed to react to her comment or not. One of the things he always loved about his relationship with Nora was that they usually seemed to be on the same page and he always seemed to know what she was thinking. But he couldn't read her this morning. *Is she just making small talk before we get to the real agenda or is there something more to the mention of Verity's recent volatility? It can't be that Noblecorp is planning to buy Verity,* he thought to himself.

Nora's tone suddenly sharpened. "I think you should go after it."

Steadfast still wasn't following her. "Go after what?"

"The Verity job. I can make a call for you."

Steadfast couldn't have been more surprised by the turn in conversation. "You want me to leave Noblecorp?" he said, wondering if she'd been unhappy somehow with his performance.

Nora smiled. "If I could hold on to you forever, I would. But we both know that you're made for something bigger. Make a move on this job. You're ready for it—and they could use you."

Nora's a genuine leader, Steadfast thought, once her advice had started to sink in. *She understands that developing the best staff and providing them with the best opportunities sometimes means preparing them so well that they have no choice but to leave. If I'm ever in her position—and maybe I will be soon—I'll need to keep that in mind.*

Over the weeks of interviews that followed, Nora had remained unwavering in her support, counseling Steadfast on strategies, helping him gain insight into key players at Verity, and debriefing with him after every stage. When the offer finally came through, Steadfast called his wife to pass along the great news, and a minute later he was in his mentor's office to share his excitement. Steadfast had quit jobs for bigger opportunities before, but he'd never experienced the enthusiasm that ensued when he told Nora. It was almost as though she'd gotten the job rather than he.

On Vince Steadfast's last day at Noblecorp, Nora had to leave his going-away party early because of an emergency at one of their subsidiaries. In that moment of celebration, Steadfast felt himself deflate. He was disappointed that they'd miss the chance to share a private good-bye. Though he knew he'd stay in close touch with Nora, he still wanted the chance to see her one last time before he headed off. When he returned to his office, though, he found a note from Nora along with the most beautiful crystal coffee cup he'd ever seen. The cup looked so delicate he was almost afraid to touch it, but when he picked it up, it felt solid in his hands, the sign of superior craftsmanship.

He turned the cup over and found the Verity insignia. The cup had obviously come from the halcyon days of invention at his new company, before they'd taken to *just* making bottles. It was probably worth a fortune, though the material value was secondary to Steadfast. That the woman who'd schooled him in so much had found this precious thing and thought to present it to him as he embarked on the most important undertaking of his life was priceless. As was the note she'd left with it, encouraging him to "keep your cup full."

Not with coffee, Nora, Steadfast thought. *This cup is much too valuable for my morning brew.*

He'd brought it with him on his first day at Verity because he planned to give it a prominent place on his desk, a constant reminder of the great leader who'd given it to him, the important lessons she'd taught him, and the extraordinary faith she'd shown in him.

As he neared the entrance, Steadfast's thoughts shifted back to the tower. It loomed large over Harken, a visual representation of the pinnacle he'd reached in his career. Nora was right; he was ready for this. And he could barely wait to get started.

Gripping the cup in his right hand, Steadfast walked to the end of the block and turned left. To his surprise, there was a size-able crowd gathered in front of the Verity building, murmuring with obvious agitation. *What is going on here?*

He made his way slowly through the crowd. Some people were attempting to make calls on their cell phones, though they didn't seem to be succeeding. Others were arguing. Many simply gaped at the tower. Steadfast had been here several times in the last month and he'd never experienced anything like this. Perhaps there had been some kind of accident.

Steadfast turned to the person nearest him, an older woman holding her cup of coffee. "Do you have any idea what's going on?"

The woman started to answer when a blaring announcement cut her short: "*Emergency! Alert! Exit the building immediately!*"

This riled the crowd further. The murmuring increased but another announcement drowned it out.

"*All employees must exit the building. Emergency! Repeat. This is an emergency.*"

The messages repeated twice, with the crowd growing visibly more agitated each time.

What a way to start my first day at a new job, Steadfast thought.

Looking around, he found a security guard who appeared to be only slightly less befuddled than the rest of the employees.

"What's happening here?" Steadfast asked. "What's the emergency?"

The guard shrugged and checked his phone before answering. "I have no idea. We were just told to exit the building so I helped clear the lobby and then got out of there. I can't get any more information. Our walkies are down, and no one is answering the emergency line."

Steadfast looped his fingers through the cup's handle so he could pull out his own phone and call the chief operating officer for some information. However, even though he was in the middle of the city, he had no service.

As the emergency message started again, Steadfast walked toward the building, though everyone else was heading the opposite way. *Kind of comes with the job description*, he thought. When he reached the lobby doors, Steadfast had a moment's recollection of the first time he had seen them. He'd been charmed by the stained glass panels with the sunburst image that was Verity's signature motif. He had no time to admire their beauty now, though, not with a restless crowd of employees—his employees—behind him.

The emergency message went silent and Steadfast turned toward the group. He tried waving his arms wildly above his head as he yelled to get everyone's attention, but it took several attempts. Finally, the crowd quieted enough for him to speak.

"My name is Vince Steadfast. As you might know, I'm the new CEO."

"Then maybe you can tell us what's going on!" someone shouted from the back of the crowd. That got the mass agitated all over again. Steadfast gestured for quiet. He was a large man, more than six feet tall with broad shoulders that had benefited him as a power forward in his college basketball days. He'd been told more than a few times that he cut an imposing figure, but his size didn't seem to be helping him much right now. It took more than a minute to calm the crowd.

"I'm afraid I don't know any more than you do, but I'm going inside to investigate."

"You can't go in there," a woman to his right shouted. "They told us to evacuate."

Steadfast nodded. "I understand that, but someone needs to find out what's happening. As the new head of the company I promise I will do my best."

There were guards posted at each of the doors, and Steadfast figured he was going to have to talk his way into the building.

The first guard he approached looked him up and down. "You're the new CEO?"

"I am."

"You know I'm not supposed to let you in there, right?"

Steadfast smiled patiently. "And you know I need to get inside, right?"

The guard nodded slowly and then stepped aside. "Good luck."

"Let's hope I don't need it."

With that, Steadfast shifted the cup to his left hand and with his right hand pulled open one of the heavy doors. He turned back to the crowd one more time, catching expressions of expectation on a number of faces. That steeled him. He hadn't even sat at his desk for the first time but the staff was already counting on him. He took a step on the marble lobby floor toward the elevators. As he did, he heard a series of thuds—the unmistakable sound of door bolts sliding into place.

Steadfast turned around. On the other side of the doors was a large crowd.

In the lobby, though, he was completely alone.

CHAPTER 2

A Blizzard of Pink Slips

Appearances, facts, and truth—how can anyone
know if they are one and the same?
—Steadfast

Only minutes ago, Steadfast had been dreaming about the exciting future he was going to have at Verity and enthusiastically anticipating his first day at work. He was looking forward to meeting a large number of the company's thousands of employees. He'd never imagined that meeting them would take place under these circumstances, though. Nor would he have guessed that he'd be looking at those employees through the glass of locked doors. Still holding the cup, he reached for the large handles with his free hand and pulled hard to confirm what he already knew. He was completely locked inside.

Alone, he turned his back to the throng and inspected the lobby. As he did, he noticed a huge flickering video screen above the abandoned reception desk. The emergency message had started again, though at this point Steadfast thought it seemed rather pointless. It appeared that all of the employees had been evacuated from the building—and if they hadn't, they were out of luck, as the exits were now impassable.

Steadfast looked skyward, trying to comprehend the surreal nature of this situation. It was going to make for some fascinating dinner conversation with his wife tonight, assuming he found a way out of the building by then. As he looked up, he realized how dim the lobby seemed. He hadn't noticed this on his earlier trips to Verity Tower, maybe because all of his interviews had happened late in the day, but now the morning light was struggling to shine through. This was especially odd because it was so sunny outside. Shouldn't that light be streaming through the crystal cupola atop the atrium, which he knew stretched some fifty stories into the sky, not to mention the glass doors? If anything, shouldn't this be one of the brightest spots in all of Harken?

That, however, was a mystery for another day. Steadfast had a bigger conundrum to deal with right now. He began to cross the marble floor, noting the majestic glass staircase that led to the mezzanine. Even in the dim light, it was a truly impressive space.

He'd taken maybe a dozen steps when he noticed something pink float past his eyes and land on the floor. Steadfast saw it was a piece of paper about the size of a postcard. As he looked down, he watched several additional pieces land nearby. And then more.

Using his free hand, he picked up a slip and read:

> **We regret to inform Ms. Cindy Pearl that her position as junior accountant at Verity Glassworks is terminated without notice, explanation, or severance.**

A pink slip? A termination notice? Steadfast reached for another:

> **We regret to inform Mr. Arthur Gold that his position as marketing manager at Verity Glassworks is terminated without notice, explanation, or severance.**

And another:

We regret to inform Ms. Judith Sheen that her position as sales associate at Verity Glassworks is terminated without notice, explanation, or severance.

Within minutes there were hundreds of pink slips littering the lobby floor and a veritable blizzard of them floating down from the top of the atrium. Did each one have the name of a different Verity staff member? Was this some kind of computer malfunction? Who used actual pink slips—or ever did—anyway, with no one even on hand to receive them? And certainly a mass firing of this sort couldn't happen without the CEO knowing about it, especially one who had just taken the job.

The onslaught of pink began to whirl in the air, as though it truly were a blizzard. People started banging on the doors, likely because of what they saw, and Steadfast pivoted back to face them. As he did, his precious glass cup slipped from his hand. If it landed on the floor, he knew it would smash into a million pieces no matter how well it had been constructed. Steadfast dropped to his knees and reached out . . . catching the cup inches from the ground.

Even though the pink slips kept falling and even though he was wearing a brand-new suit he'd bought for this occasion, Steadfast sat on the floor for a moment to catch his breath, unsure how to comprehend what was happening. He'd been sitting for perhaps ten seconds when he heard someone thumping on a microphone, the noise emanating from the speakers next to the flickering screen. It happened again, followed by the sound of someone clearing his throat.

"Good morning," a voice began, "This is the chairman of the board of directors."

Steadfast stood, glad he was finally going to get some kind of explanation for what was happening. At the same time, he saw the crowd outside shifting their attention toward what must be outdoor emergency speakers.

The chairman cleared his throat again. "It appears that we only have audio, so please listen carefully as this message is of the utmost importance. We, the board of directors, regret to inform you that Verity Glassworks has gone bankrupt."

Steadfast couldn't believe his ears.

"As the chairman, I am saddened to inform you that your positions are terminated. All work in Verity Tower is hereby cancelled. Currently, we are not able to offer an explanation and we do not have any details about your health benefits or risks to your pensions, but all matters regarding this will be looked into with perspicacity in the next one hundred days. The entire board is grateful for your service and we wish you well. As you are no longer employees and this is private property, I must ask you now to leave immediately. Thank you for your cooperation."

Steadfast could hear the roar of employees outside. They were screaming a symphony of ire at the disembodied chairman. Through the din, Steadfast could make out some individual voices.

"I have to work," a woman yelled. "I need my medical benefits. Our daughter is very sick."

Immediately, a man followed. "I'm retiring in a week. I've worked for this company for forty years. How can I retire if I might not have a pension?"

The noise of the crowd intensified. Was the suddenly jobless mass going to riot? Would they attempt to crash through the doors? Did they think Steadfast himself was party to this and that he'd actually known the building was going to lock behind him?

Not sure he could do anything to defuse the situation, he

walked toward the entrance again. "Please try to stay calm," he said, trying to project his voice. "I know you're all shocked. I'll see what I can discover."

No one seemed to even notice him.

He was about to try again when another sound came from the speakers. Steadfast turned and saw that the screen was now working and the face of chief operating officer Reed Hoggit appeared. Hoggit was one of several senior staff members he'd met with during a lavish dinner in the opulent executive lounge. Considering the food and wine they served, Steadfast would never have guessed for a second that Verity was experiencing financial problems. Nothing he'd seen in the spreadsheets they'd sent him indicated any issues either.

"Hello, my friends," Hoggit said. He looked distinguished and authoritative, if a bit overweight. "Let me assure all of you that there's nothing to worry about. I don't know why the chairman told you that Verity Glassworks is bankrupt. That is completely and utterly false."

The roar of the crowd settled down to a murmur.

Hoggit smiled widely. "I assure you that I, and all the executives here at Verity, care for each and every one of our dear, faithful employees. I know you must feel terribly shaken after the chairman's announcement, and I can appreciate how this has affected you. I'd therefore like all of you to go home and relax. I'm declaring today a paid holiday for everyone."

The crowd was cheering now. Steadfast could hear several employees expressing faith in their executives. The sense of relief was palpable, even through the heavy glass doors. Steadfast watched as the mass began to disperse quickly.

It seemed odd to him that they were so completely convinced they could rely on what Hoggit said. He was the financial and operations guy, not the person who led the company or the board.

Though Hoggit might understand the numbers, he couldn't possibly have all the inside information on the fate of the company. Appearances, facts, and truth; how could anyone know if they were one and the same?

Of course, Steadfast, who was the actual boss—at least in title—was the person who should be communicating company-wide information, but he had no idea about *anything* that was going on. Obviously, there was a critical rift in the management of the company.

Maybe there was more than he thought behind the numerous changes in CEOs over the past few years—but what? During the interview process he had rationalized it as being due to decisions the board had made when hiring flashy executives—those who were looking to add the luster of the Verity brand to their résumés without having the actual experience of running a traditional, old-fashioned manufacturing company. Lots of leaders today didn't have any experience making real things, and maybe they lacked an understanding of the people who actually made them.

Steadfast moved away from the doors and walked back through the lobby, his shoes submerged under all the pink slips.

If everything is okay, as Hoggit says, then what are these all about?

That was one of the many things he needed to find out. He headed toward the elevator bank in hope that he'd get the answers he needed on the executive floor.

That's when the lights went out.

CHAPTER 3

A Good Place to Begin the Quest

I know you'll get to the truth…and then act
on it.

—Elevator operator

Stopping, Steadfast stood in near darkness. With the power out, the dimness was eerie. He couldn't understand why a building of this size, with a factory attached, wouldn't have backup generators. He could add that to the rapidly growing list of questions he needed answered once he found Hoggit and any other members of the executive team he could locate. Despite the evacuation order, he assumed that they were still in the building because of the announcements, though maybe they were in different places, since Hoggit had video and the chairman didn't—and they were completely contradicting each other.

How was he going to get to them? There had to be a fire stairway somewhere in the lobby. Steadfast started trudging through the slips to find it. If he'd known he'd be taking the staircase to the executive floor, he would have worn more comfortable shoes.

He'd taken only a few steps when a mechanical whir sounded behind him. The elevators? How could the elevators be working when all of the power was out? Shaking his head at yet another mystery, he turned and headed toward the sound.

Indeed, one of the elevators seemed to be moving. He could

tell because the floor number was lit above the door. Well, not a number, actually. It was a symbol shaped like the crystal cupola that crowned Verity Tower. Another thing he hadn't noticed on any of his earlier visits.

The whirring grew louder, and the elevator doors slid open. The inside of the cabin had plenty of light, and Steadfast saw a refined-looking older woman standing there. He stepped back to allow her to exit, but she waved him in. He stepped inside, still looking at the woman. She was wearing what appeared to be a uniform of slate blue. It consisted of a pleated jacket with a double row of brass buttons and a skirt that nearly touched the ground. The woman wore her gray hair pinned up with a round hat on top of her head. If this were 1938, she would have looked perfectly appropriate.

"Good morning, Mr. Steadfast."

Steadfast startled; he'd been preoccupied with thoughts about the woman and he was surprised to hear his name.

"You know who I am?"

"You're the new CEO, Vince Steadfast. Of course I know who you are."

The way she said it made Steadfast feel surprisingly welcome. There'd of course been announcements of his hiring in the newspapers, online and in the trades, but it still gave him a bit of a charge to think that anyone would recognize him on his first day. "Thanks," was all he could think to say.

"Which floor can I take you to?"

That seemed like an odd question. "Take me to?"

The woman offered a mild chuckle. "Well, I *am* the elevator operator. I wouldn't be very good at my job if I couldn't take you where you wanted to go." She leaned toward him and whispered. "And a little secret? The elevator does all the work."

Elevator operator? Steadfast had no memory of elevator

operators in this building from his previous trips here. That wasn't the sort of thing he would have forgotten. After all, how many buildings had them any longer? They'd been made obsolete by cost cutting and automation—sort of like the artisanal glass sculptures that once defined the company itself.

"That's a beautiful cup you have there, Mr. Steadfast," the woman said when he failed to speak.

Steadfast looked down at the cup and tilted it toward her. "This? Thanks. It's great, isn't it? My mentor gave it to me yesterday."

"It's a beauty. We made that, didn't we?"

Steadfast noted she used the word "we." He considered it a good sign—maybe the first of the day—that the elevator operator identified so closely with Verity. "Yes. Yes, this was made by Verity a long time ago."

"A very long time ago, I would guess. Back when we were making such things. Part of our extremely proud past. Have you tried pinging it?"

"Pinging?"

"You know—" She gestured a flick with her thumb and index finger.

"Oh, I don't want to do anything that might hurt it. It was a very special gift and, you know, it's glass."

The woman smiled again. "You're not going to hurt it, I promise. Verity glass is very sturdy stuff, especially from back then. Give it a ping."

Not certain why he felt so reassured, Steadfast pinged the cup. It rang out as though amplified; the ring resonated for much longer than he ever would have guessed. Steadfast found himself grinning. When he looked at the woman, he saw she was doing the same.

"We made remarkable things years ago," she said.

"I can see that. I wonder where Nora got this. It came with a note that read, 'Always keep your cup full and your life will overflow with joy.' Of course I don't plan on drinking my coffee in it, though I was kind of looking forward to my first cup this morning. But clearly nothing is routine today."

"Thirteenth floor, then?"

Steadfast nodded. "Yes, thirteenth floor. Do you know if the others are there?"

The woman hit 13 on the control panel. "I can't say for certain."

"I need to have a talk with the chairman and the others. I need to make sense of what has been going on this morning. Did you hear the announcements?"

"I did. Very upsetting. I must say it shook me to my core."

It dawned on Steadfast that the woman was supposed to have left with everyone else. "Shouldn't you be taking your free vacation day?"

The woman's eyes flickered but Steadfast couldn't read them. "It's better if I stay at my post."

He wasn't sure what to make of that. "The doors are locked now, anyway," he said. Again, he shook his head. *How many times had he done that already this morning?*

"No one said anything to me about any of this when I was interviewing for the job. There's something incredibly wrong and I need to get to the bottom of it, for all of us."

The woman's eyes flickered again, but this time there was a brightness to them that Steadfast interpreted as pride...in him. At that moment, Steadfast caught a similar brilliance coming from his cup. When he looked down, he was amazed to see bright light slowly etching a word in beautiful script into the glass next to the handle. It startled him so much he nearly dropped the cup for the second time that morning.

Surprisingly, the elevator operator steadied his hand and the two made momentary eye contact. Then they both looked down at the cup again. The light was gone, but as Steadfast inspected the cup he noticed that the word RESPONSIBILITY was visible on the outside. It looked just like the message on an inspirational gift he might give to someone on his team. He loved those kinds of things—but this one was much more beautiful. Steadfast ran his thumb across the letters; they were still warm.

"It appears that your cup appreciates the fact you want to do what's best for your staff," the elevator operator said.

Steadfast was still mesmerized by the magic trick that had just happened, but the woman had raised a subject that meant a great deal to him.

"Well, of course," he said. "You can't really call yourself a leader if you aren't willing to put what's best for your team first."

"There are some here who might not agree with that senti-ment," she said darkly. Then her eyes glimmered again and she nodded toward the cup. "Look what's inside."

Steadfast tilted the cup toward him and his eyes opened wide. What he saw was a drop of golden elixir resting at the bottom. He could swear the liquid had a glow of its own, and he knew for a fact it hadn't been there earlier.

"Where'd that come from?" he said, instinctively glancing up at the ceiling, as though something had dripped from there.

"My guess is that it came from the same place the etched word came from."

"And where would that be?"

Her expression grew bemused. "I really can't say," she said with the hint of a smile.

Steadfast shifted the cup. The liquid balled up, but it didn't run, no matter what angle he tried. Another mystery.

Just then, the elevator stopped and the doors slid open.

"Here you are at the thirteenth floor, Mr. Steadfast. A good place to begin the quest."

"The quest? You mean to find out what's going on?"

"Yes, that too." The woman tipped her head forward slightly. "I know you'll get to the truth . . . and then act on it."

This easily qualified as the strangest elevator ride of Steadfast's life. "Any suggestions on how to accomplish this?" he said, joking.

The woman locked eyes with him, with a slightly furrowed brow. "You need to find the Treasure Beyond All Price."

Steadfast was so baffled he didn't even realize he'd stepped out of the elevator. He only noticed he was standing on the thirteenth floor when the doors shut.

You need to find the Treasure Beyond All Price. Who said things like that?

Looking down the hall, Steadfast contemplated his "quest."

CHAPTER 4

Legends and Treasures

Companies could crumble because frightened
or misguided leadership forgot where they came
from and what their core purpose really was.
—Steadfast

Steadfast headed down the darkened hall to the chairman's
office but found it empty. Next, he went to Hoggit's office, two
suites away, guided by the bit of light coming from the windows.
Again, no one was to be seen, not even an executive assistant.
His own new office was on the other side of the hall, but he didn't
even bother to go there, as he knew what he would find—his
own empty executive suite with an abandoned desk where his
assistant should be in high gear for his arrival. In fact, the entire
floor seemed deserted. If no one was here, from where had the
conflicting announcements come?

Maybe the company's top management (minus himself, of
course) was gathered in the executive conference room. That
would certainly explain things, though it didn't sync with his
theory of the broadcasts coming from different places. Steadfast
turned the corner and walked toward the boardroom. Less than
a week ago, he'd had his last meeting for his new position in that
very room. The future seemed so incredibly bright then. It had

seemed so bright even *an hour ago*. How could things have suddenly turned so ominous?

Steadfast reached the boardroom's ornate double doors. He
could hear what seemed like hushed conversation coming from
the other side, though he couldn't make out anything that was
being said. He turned the knob only to find the door locked, so
he knocked. The voices continued uninterrupted.

Steadfast knocked again. "Hello? Mr. Chairman? Reed? It's
Vince Steadfast. I assume you've been expecting me."

Steadfast waited for the door to open, but nothing happened.
He could still hear muffled conversation, as though his presence
was being actively ignored.

He knocked again. "As you can imagine," he said raising his
voice, "I'm very concerned about the announcements this morning. I'd appreciate it if you would let me in so I can participate in
whatever is going on."

Again, his request went completely unheeded. This was
unnerving. He was the CEO but did he even have a job? If the
company had actually gone bankrupt, would Nora take him
back?

Just then, a door opened at the end of the hall. A man emerged
who appeared to be in his sixties with a mess of gray hair and a
bushy mustache. He turned toward Steadfast and tilted his head
as though he were looking at a rare beast in the jungle.

"You are . . ." the man said.

Steadfast took a few steps in the man's direction. "My name is
Vince Steadfast."

He seemed to register this very slowly. "The new CEO?"

"Yes. Would you by any chance know how I can get into the
boardroom? The doors are locked and I need to be in on whatever meeting is happening there now."

The man's bushy brows knit together. "You don't want to be in there."

"I think I do. I think I *need* to." Steadfast's mind flashed on the word RESPONSIBILITY etched into his cup.

The man shook his head quickly. "The board is not the answer, I guarantee you." He stuck out his hand. "Let me introduce myself. I'm Professor Reposit. I've been employed here as the corporate librarian and historian since I left my teaching post at Yale more than twenty years ago."

"It's very nice to meet you, professor. I do feel the need to get into that boardroom, though."

The professor sighed slowly. "You really don't." He gestured toward the doorway he'd just left. "Why don't you come into my library? Maybe I can help you with what you're looking for."

Steadfast doubted it, unless the professor was updating the history of the company on an hourly basis. Still, he decided to follow the man inside. When he did, he became even more dubious. Every available space in the library was crammed with books, binders, tapes, DVDs, and every other storage device imaginable. Were those eight-inch floppies? There were massive piles everywhere. If there was an organizing system to this, Steadfast guessed that only the professor knew what it was.

And then there were the candles. Maybe a dozen of different sizes were burning on top of a variety of surfaces where stacks of papers and objects had been pushed aside. Since the power was out and there were no windows in the library, the candles were the only source of light.

"Fortunately, I always keep plenty of these at the ready," Reposit said, obviously following Steadfast's line of vision. "You never know when the electricity is just going to disappear. I mean, can we really trust technology at all?" He pointed toward his computer. "I've seen years of work vanish in a wink. Haven't you?"

Steadfast hadn't. He'd always been a stickler for backing up his data. He was guessing the professor hadn't heard about the cloud, where everyone's data was now stored and shared forever. Clearly, that was a policy he'd have to institute at Verity, assuming he got to institute *any* policies here. "Why didn't you leave when the emergency alarm went off?"

The professor tilted his head again and then shook it swiftly. "I didn't hear any alarm."

"It was very loud downstairs. It's hard to believe you could have missed it."

Reposit seemed to consider this for a moment, then said, "I might have been lost in my reading. I was catching up on an old biography about the founder."

"The founder?"

"Crystal Modello. The founder of Verity Glassworks."

Steadfast had come across the name when he was doing background research on Verity. "Yes, of course."

"One of the truly great visionary leaders. She built Verity Tower and kept the company at a creative peak for decades. Her story is fascinating. You see, Crystal Modello came from Murano, the famous glass-making island in Italy and—"

"I don't mean to be rude, professor, but I'm going to have to ask you to give me this story some other time. If you didn't hear the alarm, I'm guessing you also didn't hear the announcements from the chairman and Reed Hoggit. The chairman announced that the company has gone bankrupt. Hoggit refuted it and sent everyone home with what he called a paid vacation day to make up for all the turmoil. But then there were all these pink slips and—"

"Verity is bankrupt?"

"Well, it either is or it isn't, depending on who you listen to. I was discussing this with the elevator operator—"

"We don't have any elevator operators."

"I didn't think so, either, but an elevator operator—an elegant woman—very definitely brought me up to this floor."

Reposit scoffed. "I would know if we had elevator operators. There haven't been any in this building for more than half a century. I did mention that I'm the corporate historian, didn't I?"

"Yes, you did. However, there very definitely was an operator in the elevator this morning, though I have to admit she was a little mysterious. She was very curious about my cup." Steadfast held it out to Reposit. "And as I was getting off, she told me that I needed to find the Treasure Beyond All Price. I don't have the slightest idea what she was talking about."

The professor stared in silence.

"I'm guessing you *do* have an idea what she's talking about," Steadfast said when Reposit didn't share his thoughts.

"Not entirely, but for the past few months Mr. Hoggit has been searching the library for any information about just such a treasure."

"Really?"

"Indeed. Of course, I helped him in whatever way I could. Mr. Hoggit has always shown so much interest in my work. He was one of the first readers of my latest volume."

Reposit patted a thick leather journal sitting on an oak table next to him. Steadfast leaned forward and read the title: A *Brief Compendium on the Legend of the Founder, including the Origin of the Worthy Way, the Crystal Cupola, and Related Topics, Volume Three.* That was quite a title.

Steadfast looked at the professor. "The legend of the founder?"

Reposit seemed to warm to this. "And quite a legend it is. As I mentioned, Crystal Modello built Verity Tower. She designed the atrium that stretches from the lobby to the crystal cupola atop the marble dome, some five hundred feet above the ground.

Light once poured through the cupola, filling the building with its brilliance."

Steadfast considered this, remembering how dark the lobby had seemed to him this morning. "What happened?"

"No one really knows—not even me, which is saying something. My research has suggested that after the founder died, a corrupt CEO sealed off the cupola."

"Why would anyone do that?"

Reposit shrugged. "Fear? Control? Desire to take things in a new direction, even though the old direction had served the company remarkably well? Verity has been slowly dimming ever since. Maybe we really have come to the point of bankruptcy. It wouldn't be completely out of the realm of possibility."

Once again, Steadfast's head was spinning, though some of what Reposit was saying made sense to him. He'd seen companies crumble when frightened or misguided leadership forgot where they came from and what their core business and purpose really was. "I can't believe the board concealed this all from me. I mean, I knew they'd gone through several CEOs in the past few years, but I had no idea conditions were this bad."

The professor chuckled. "I can believe they held out on you. This is not the most virtuous lot. They probably figured you wouldn't take the job if you knew how awful things were. The other recent CEOs before you seemed happy to defer, especially to Hoggit, who has been positioning himself behind the scenes for a while. In fact, I thought Hoggit had finally succeeded and I was surprised—pleasantly, I might say—that you were appointed."

Steadfast felt unease creeping up his spine. He tightened his grip on his cup and then thought of the woman who'd given it to him. Nora was so tuned in to the business world in Harken she would have had some inkling this was going on at Verity. But she couldn't have, because if she did, she never would have encouraged him to go after the job. Nora was the kind of leader who always looked after her people, and she wouldn't have guided him into an untenable and possibly corrupt environment. Or would she? Did she know something he still didn't? He'd have to keep an open mind.

"I'm still not following why anyone would seal off the cupola," he said. "What was there to be afraid of?"

The professor rose to the topic. "According to legend, the founder left a dangerous treasure up there."

This was all getting too mystical for Steadfast. "You're about to tell me that this is the Treasure Beyond All Price, right?"

"That's what I'm thinking now. I've been finding clues."

"Okay, even if that's the case, why is it dangerous?"

Reposit slumped a bit. "I don't know. But it had to be something the company's subsequent leaders feared."

Steadfast couldn't believe he was thinking this way, but the elevator operator had mentioned a "quest." He assumed she was just using flowery language to describe the fact-finding he had in front of him. But maybe she was talking about an actual *Lord of the Rings*–style quest. "If I could get to the cupola…"

The professor sighed. "Yes, I know. I've checked every inch of the top floor, and I've found no way to reach the cupola. But based on everything I've learned over the years about the founder, I'm convinced that she created a secret route, something that would lead to the treasure. There are hints in some of her later correspondence about something called the Worthy Way. I haven't been able to find that, either, but I believe I know where it begins."

Though he'd been working for Verity for less than an hour, Steadfast found himself caught up in the notion that there was something hidden in the building that could reverse the company's fortunes. Always the person who took things at face value, he was the least likely person to believe in magical quests, but the events of the morning had left him less sure about everything. "Professor, I think it's my mission to find the Treasure Beyond All Price."

At that moment, Steadfast jumped. His cup had come alive again! This time, the word CURIOSITY glowed and then slowly etched itself on the outside surface, just below the word RESPONSIBILITY. When Steadfast looked into the cup, he saw even more golden elixir pooling on the bottom.

Steadfast was more curious than ever. He certainly had an ever-growing need to find out what was going on at Verity and to seek out the source of the problems before things got worse. And he also had an increasing sense of fascination with this special cup and all the oddities that kept coming at him. It was unnerving...but also more than a little exhilarating.

"Fascinating," the professor said brightly.

"That's one word for it." Steadfast closed his eyes for a moment, still seeing the afterimage of CURIOSITY on the cup. He looked at the professor. "Where do you think the Worthy Way begins?"

"I'm nearly certain it starts in a place the legends call the 'Perilous Passage.' As far as I've been able to determine, it's located somewhere in the portrait gallery on the mezzanine."

Steadfast turned toward the door. "Then that's where I'll go."

"Very well," the professor said, stuffing *A Brief Compendium* into a battered leather satchel and picking up a candle. He stepped toward Steadfast. "Let's be on our way."

Steadfast hadn't actually planned on bringing Reposit along with him. However, something told him that convincing the professor to stay behind might be tougher than finding the secret entrance to the cupola.

"Yes, let's go. We need to make one stop first."

CHAPTER 5

A Clue from the Gallery

"Faster and easier" was good in the short term, and our old reputation held up for a surprisingly long time.

—Professor Reposit

Slowly, Steadfast and the professor made their way down the hallway. Though the strangeness of the morning was foremost in his mind, Steadfast couldn't help but notice the impressive surroundings. Even in the dim light, it was clear that the executive floor had been appointed lavishly with artwork and artifacts from around the world. Whatever was going on financially with Verity, they made a real effort to project a positive outward appearance. Had the expensive décor actually contributed to their troubles, or was it the kind of thing that could inspire a turnaround? Steadfast hoped he'd be working in the building long enough to find out.

Steadfast reminded Reposit that they had a stop to make before they could set off on their mission. He needed to make one more effort to get into the boardroom. Regardless of the circumstances, it wasn't acceptable that the board was meeting without him. If he couldn't participate in righting the ship, how could he possibly take the helm as CEO with any hope of succeeding?

They got to the huge double doors. Again, Steadfast could hear voices inside, though they were just barely audible. And again he tried the knob and the door was still locked. He banged hard. And then a little harder.

"I'm going to break down the door," he said to Reposit.

"Well, that would be dramatic. And probably cause for termination."

Steadfast considered this. In his entire professional life, he'd never done anything as reckless as what he was contemplating now.

He stepped back and rammed the door.

Which turned out to be considerably sturdier than he'd expected. Steadfast imagined this was what running headlong into concrete felt like. He slumped against the door for a moment.

"They built things very solidly back then," Reposit said.

"You aren't kidding."

Without thinking about it, Steadfast drew back and slammed into the door again. He felt it shake a little this time, but it still didn't budge. It was becoming increasingly clear that the only thing likely to break in this scenario was his shoulder.

Steadfast took a deep breath and closed his eyes, resigned. He opened them to see Reposit holding something in his other hand—a lock tumbler.

"This popped out," the professor said, before he dropped it into his pocket. "You're very strong."

He tried the door again, and this time it opened...into an empty boardroom. There were signs of recent activity, including a video camera and a microphone, but no one was there. The voices were more distinct now. They were coming from a laptop running a video playback of a board meeting. Watching it for a minute, Steadfast quickly realized the video had not been recorded today. First, Kacen, the previous CEO, was on the recording. Second, the conversation had nothing to do with the announcements this morning.

Steadfast looked over at Reposit. "I'm completely confused."

"I told you that you couldn't count on the board for anything. It always came across to me that their heads were in the sand. When things were bad, they just seemed to ignore it."

Steadfast clicked off the laptop and they left the boardroom. When they got to the elevators, he pressed the down button.

"What makes you think an elevator is going to come?" Reposit said. "There's no power, remember?"

Steadfast pressed the button again. "I took an elevator up here, remember?"

The professor nodded broadly. "Oh, yes, when you met the *elevator operator.*"

Steadfast didn't appreciate the sarcasm, but he let it pass. He was about to press the button a third time, but he stopped himself. Reposit was right; the elevators were as devoid of electrical power as the rest of the building.

"The stairs don't require electricity," the professor said, pointing to a door next to the elevator. "Truly elegant technology. I just hope my old knees hold up."

Steadfast nodded and gestured for Reposit to lead the way. They headed down the staircase as quickly as the candlelight and the professor's legs would allow.

Finally, they reached a door that read: MEZZANINE: VERITY PORTRAIT GALLERY

They stepped onto the balcony that ringed the soaring atrium. A little bit of outside light filtered in, but the professor refused to extinguish his candle, which Steadfast thought was a bit foolhardy; they had no idea how long the power was going to stay out, and the candle was only going to burn for so long. Steadfast had thought about using his cell phone flashlight, but for the same reason he thought it was prudent to keep it off as long as possible.

Steadfast watched as Reposit looked down at the lobby from the balcony and waved his hand at the sea of pink slips. "Are those..."

"They are."

"This is not good."

With a slight shudder, the professor turned toward the gallery. "Here are the best of us," he said with a note of melancholy in his voice.

Steadfast had worked for companies that honored their pasts, but never with such a respectful canonizing of their former leaders. Each painting was a carefully rendered oil that wouldn't seem out of place in a nation's embassy or capitol. The juxtaposition against the clutter of pink just a floor below was chilling.

Steadfast studied the full-length portrait of a Mrs. Keane. She looked regal, wearing a golden gown and a black-plumed hat. The painting was terribly old-fashioned, but at the same time inspiring. It was obvious from the image that Keane knew she was part of an organization that mattered.

The professor stood next to him and pointed. "See those glass sculptures in the background?"

"They're beautiful."

"You have a talent for understatement. Those are early pieces from Verity Glassworks. The artisans used a wax mold technique that required years of apprenticeship to master."

Steadfast leaned closer. "Did they look in real life the way they do in this painting?"

"Very much so."

"It's incredible. That swan—look at how its feathers are touched by the wind. And look at how the unicorn's wings catch the light."

"I've been fortunate enough to see one of the unicorn pieces in person. It was named *Winged Defender*. It might be the most beautiful sculpture we've ever produced."

There's that word we *again*, Steadfast thought. "Stunning. Really."

Reposit stepped away from the painting. "And now we make bottles."

Steadfast turned toward him. "Bottles can be beautiful as well."

The professor grunted. "They can be, but our bottles are purely functional. I think the most elegant thing we churn out these days is something used for extra-virgin olive oil."

Steadfast looked back at Keane again. Her upturned chin had nothing to do with the company's success at creating olive oil bottles. "When did Verity stop making such beautiful works of art?"

Reposit had moved on to another painting, studying the image as though he'd never seen it before. "It began after Crystal Modello was gone. There were faster and easier ways to make money with condiment and beverage bottles, and new generations of leadership embraced those. It was good in the short term, and our old reputation held up for a surprisingly long time. People still thought of Verity as a manufacturer of fine crystal long after they'd stopped making pieces like *Winged Defender* or that cup you're holding."

Steadfast looked down at his cup. The rim gleamed, though there was no direct light on it. He checked the golden liquid inside to make sure it hadn't dripped out during the descent from the thirteenth floor. It was all still there.

The professor stepped away from the painting and looked out at the atrium. "Amazingly enough, people still think fondly of Verity. Maybe things have finally caught up to us, though," Reposit added. "Come on, let me introduce you to Crystal."

They walked past several paintings until they reached the portrait of a stately woman with rich auburn hair, standing at the bottom of the glass stairs in the lobby. She held a clear goblet in her raised hand that glinted with a similar spark of light Steadfast had just seen on his coffee cup. A selection of Verity's sculptures was placed artfully on the stairs and in the background.

As with the other portraits, Crystal's expression was both confident and proud. There was something that stood out in her image, though: certitude in her eyes. Steadfast sensed a belief in her work that he assumed extended to the products Verity created and the people she'd entrusted to make them.

"She's exactly where she wants to be," Steadfast said.

"From everything I've read about her, that was always the case. This company was *her*."

Steadfast had been looking at the various sculptures in the painting. When he looked at Crystal Modello again, he felt a little jolt.

"She looks so familiar," he said.

"I'm sure you encountered her image many times while you were doing your due diligence. I've often wished I could have met her, but she died long before I ever stepped foot in Verity Tower."

Something else caught Steadfast's eye now. "Professor, there, engraved on her goblet. Is that an image of the crystal cupola?"

Holding his candle away from him, Reposit leaned closer to the painting. "Yes, I believe it is."

Steadfast unfastened his belt, looped the handle of his cup through it, and then refastened the buckle. He needed both hands free for what he was going to do next. He ran his fingers along the frame of Crystal's portrait, expecting something that would offer a clue to access the path the professor had mentioned. What had he called it? *The Worthy Way.*

Nothing.

"I see what you're doing. I have examined, pinged, and pressed most of this gallery in my long search for the Perilous Passage," Reposit said. "I've never found what I was looking for."

Steadfast locked eyes with Crystal's painted ones. She seemed to be trying to tell him something. Without thinking, he reached out and touched her raised goblet.

"You can't!" the professor said. "You'll damage the glaze!"

Suddenly, the mahogany panel holding the canvas groaned and fell toward them. Steadfast jumped back, grabbing the professor's arm.

When the panel landed softly on the floor, Steadfast peered underneath to make sure the painting was undamaged. The molding seemed perfectly designed to protect it. Then he stood and moved toward the space where the painting had once been.

A dark opening loomed before them.

CHAPTER 6

An Easier Way?

He had a responsibility that superseded all others—to do what was best for the company and to do it with the least amount of risk.

—Steadfast

Steadfast stared deep into the hole in the wall. Was this truly the beginning of the Worthy Way? He'd barely heard of such a thing and now he believed it was the key to his, and the entire company's, future. Was he losing his mind, or opening it in some way that would be important for their success?

The professor was standing next to him, their shoulders touching. Steadfast took a quick glance at Reposit and saw that he seemed dumbfounded as well by this latest turn of events. Steadfast dug into his jacket pocket and turned on his cell phone flashlight, which he extended into the hole. He could make out metal rungs that stretched up and out of sight, but little else.

"The Perilous Passage," the professor said in a voice lacking most of its usual timbre. Even as stunned as Steadfast felt, he found it comical how awestruck Reposit seemed. "After all these years to have found the Worthy Way. I must be dreaming."

Steadfast clapped the professor on the shoulder. "Let's find out what's on the other side."

Steadfast had just begun to climb through the hole in the wall when he heard the sound of quick footsteps from the direction of the glass stairway. Both men turned toward the approaching sound.

Within seconds, a security guard appeared. She was short and stocky, with a long blond ponytail. And she seemed very agitated.

"What on earth do you think you're doing?" she said. "This is destruction of valuable property, and in the middle of a crisis! Did you really think you could get away with this looting?"

Steadfast held up both hands in an effort to calm the guard. "It's not like that at all. I can explain everything. We're—"

Suddenly, the guard's expression changed to one of surprise. "Are you the...new CEO?"

Steadfast lowered his hands. "I am, yes."

"I'm so sorry, sir. I meant no disrespect."

"None taken." Steadfast reached out a hand. "I'm Vince Steadfast."

The guard seemed too rattled to shake Steadfast's hand. "Of course you are. Again, I apologize, Mr. Steadfast, sir." She looked down at her own hands for a moment and then saluted. "Sergeant Ernesta Stout, sir."

Sergeant, Steadfast thought. *No one mentioned that Verity employed its own army, though at this point I suppose anything is possible. Maybe she served before taking this job.* Regardless, he found himself instinctively returning her salute, though he managed to stop himself before his hand got to his forehead. Instead, he bowed toward her. "It's good to meet you, Sergeant Stout. Why don't you let me explain what we're doing here."

Steadfast did exactly that for the next several minutes. The professor of course felt the need to interject regularly. He'd pulled out his *Brief Compendium* and used it to back up what Steadfast was telling the guard. Stout seemed to take it all in, nodding sharply several times. When Steadfast was finished, and Reposit was done underlining what Steadfast had just said, Stout adopted a parade rest pose.

"Permission to speak freely, Mr. Steadfast, sir," she said.

Steadfast had to chuckle. "I'm not your commanding officer, Sergeant Stout. You always have permission to speak freely."

"Thank you, sir. I've been working here for a few years now, and I've heard stories about the dangerous treasure hidden in the crystal cupola. In my opinion, it's nonsense."

"Nonsense?" said the professor. "Well, I'll have you know that—"

Steadfast stopped him. "Please, professor. Let's listen to what the sergeant has to say." He gestured for her to continue.

"I'm willing to admit that maybe there's *something* to this treasure story." She looked briefly at Reposit before returning her gaze to Steadfast. "But why go on such a crazy search when there's an easier way to save the company?"

Steadfast was intrigued. "I'm listening."

Stout leaned toward the two men as though she was about to impart the darkest of mysteries. "There's the secret company vault."

Steadfast probably should have been accustomed to surprises by now, but he hadn't gotten to that point just yet. "There is?"

"Yes, sir. It's down in the factory, and several people have told me that it contains Verity's most valuable assets, though none of these people have seen the assets themselves. Everyone seems to think that there are stocks and bonds piled to the ceiling in that room. I know exactly where it is, and I can take you there."

"Now *this* is nonsense!" said the professor. "In all of my studies—and I promise both of you that no one alive knows more about this company and this building than I do—I have never seen a single reference to a secret vault, not to mention a secret cache of stocks and bonds."

"Maybe some things are above your pay grade, professor," Stout said in a serious tone. Reposit sputtered while the sergeant addressed Steadfast once again. "If this is about money, according to the rumors, there's more money down there than you could possibly need to turn our company around."

Steadfast tried to make sense of it all. If what Stout was saying were true, it certainly would be easier to pull out this secret collection of stocks and bonds. If they had been down there for a long time, they could be worth a small fortune, given how big Verity had grown over the years and how many times the original stock had split. He considered what the elevator operator had said about the Treasure Beyond All Price and how the professor seemed to reinforce it. But could any journey that began on something called the "Perilous Passage" lead to a happy ending?

He walked back over to the hole in the wall and shined his cell phone flashlight into it. Could this really lead to the crystal cupola? And if so, was there really a treasure up there? There was something very romantic about it, and Steadfast loved the idea of being the guy who could restore Verity's old luster. However, as CEO, he had a responsibility that superseded all others, to do what was best for the company and to do it with the least amount of risk.

He clicked off his flashlight and turned toward Stout and Reposit. "Sergeant, please lead us to this secret vault."

The professor gestured wildly. "How could you be listening to her? You know what we're supposed to be doing. We're supposed to be taking the Worthy Way, not the *easy* way."

Steadfast listened to Reposit's rant; it did cause him to reconsider for a moment. The professor made a good point about their mission, but then Steadfast chose prudence. "I understand your concerns, professor, but we're going to give this a try first."

He motioned for Stout to lead on, and as they began to walk

Steadfast tightened the knot on his tie and straightened his jacket, feeling more like an executive than he had since he'd entered the building this morning. As he did, his crystal cup jangled against his belt. He looked down and he could see the golden elixir inside. There seemed to be less of it, though. Nothing he'd done so far had made the liquid spill. Did he do something now to jostle it loose? He looked behind him to see if he was leaving a trail of gold, but he couldn't find anything.

As they made their way down the glass staircase, Steadfast felt as though he were descending on air. Verity really had been a place of endless wonders at one time, hadn't it?

When they reached the bottom, they made a sharp turn down a short hallway toward the factory wing.

"Have you had a tour of the factory already, Mr. Steadfast?" Stout said.

"Yes, during the interview process."

"Then I don't need to remind you of the dangers—the extreme heat, the molten liquid, the need to keep your hands at your sides and not touch anything..."

"No, I understand, I'm aware of them."

They stopped at a tall metal door and Stout pulled it open. The heat from the room hit them with force. Steadfast had forgotten how hot it was in the factory, especially without the state-of-the-art ventilation system that obviously wasn't working because of the power failure.

Stout led them deeper into the factory. As beads of sweat broke out on Steadfast's brow, his worry mounted.

CHAPTER 7

Transformation

Everyone was going to have to be part of the 'we' of the organization. There was no room for a "me" organization.

—Steadfast

As they walked, Steadfast considered the surroundings. A high upper wall of windows, designed like a church nave, lighted the cavernous factory. Yellow ladders enclosed in cages crawled up the walls. Catwalks crisscrossed the ceiling, stretching from one end of the building to the other. Steadfast guessed that on a normal day the factory would be clattering with the symphonic sounds of production. He imagined a swirl of activity: machinery operating, motors running, colleagues directing one another and sharing the occasional joke. On a normal day this factory would be buzzing like the main street of a small city. But today was not a normal day.

"That's not good," Stout said, pointing to a large piece of industrial equipment. "There must be a hole in the mixer. Look at all the sand and soda ash on the ground."

Steadfast noticed what seemed to be a leak in the huge machine. "This is where the raw ingredients begin processing?"

Stout nodded. "Yep. We call it the batch. This equipment is usually in great shape and it's inspected all the time."

She shook her head slowly and then continued to lead them forward. "You're probably going to want to take off your jacket, Mr. Steadfast. It's gonna get pretty warm in here."

"Warmer than it already is?"

"It's pretty intense at the hot end."

There was a *hotter* end? The tour Steadfast had been given earlier had been a cursory one—like so much of the interview process, it turned out—and he hadn't gone past the first few pieces of machinery. He remembered it was warm but not nearly as warm as it felt right now.

At last, they reached the furnace, an enormous brick box raised above the factory floor. Despite Stout's suggestion, Steadfast had kept his jacket on—he'd always had a thing about being properly dressed at work—but he was realizing he might need to relent. He took a step closer to the furnace.

"You're going to want to be very careful around this thing," the sergeant said. "There's four hundred tons of molten glass in that furnace at four hundred and fifty degrees Celsius."

Steadfast thought about the men and women who worked under these conditions daily. They had to be an awfully dedicated crew.

"Since the power is out, shouldn't the furnace be cooling down?" he said.

The professor blew out his candle and finally broke his silence. "That much molten glass would take weeks to cool—at least to cool enough for you to notice."

Before Steadfast had a chance to linger, the sergeant waved them on. Soon, they came upon the production lines. Steadfast had seen video of these lines alive with golden flashes of molten glass filling forms and cooling quickly into the bottles that generated the overwhelming majority of Verity's income. The entire process seemed somewhat fanciful to him, even though he understood the science. The bottles Verity made now were nothing like the works of art they had created in another era, but they were still the product of a remarkable act of transformation. Steadfast vowed to make regular trips to the factory floor, assuming, of course, the factory ever awakened again and he was around to see it.

They continued walking, the air cooling ever so slightly as they moved farther from the furnace. After a few minutes, Stout knelt by a concrete patch that bore a repeating pattern similar to the sunburst image he'd seen on Verity's entry doors. "Here's the vault," she said.

Steadfast looked at the professor and then back at Stout. "I don't see anything."

"You don't see anything," Reposit said, "because there's nothing to see. The *sergeant* has been imagining all of this."

Stout stared at the professor narrowly and then unsnapped one of the many pockets on her jacket. She pulled out a ring of keys that was even bigger than the one she wore on her belt.

"The crew said these might come in handy at some point," she said. She looked at the ground, examining it, and then back at the ring. She chose a thick H key and inserted it into a barely visible hole in the floor. This caused a latch to pop up, and with great effort Stout heaved open what turned out to be a concrete door. Again, she glared at the professor, who, Steadfast noticed, had taken to studying his shoes.

The sergeant pulled out her flashlight and aimed the beam into the darkness. Steadfast moved closer to the opening to see a ladder stretching downward.

"Excellent work," came a voice from behind them.

Steadfast pivoted to see Reed Hoggit standing there. The man's eyes seemed unnaturally intense and he had a half grin, half sneer on his face. For some reason, Steadfast noticed that the COO had not shaven, which was odd because he was otherwise impeccably dressed.

"Guard, what is your name?" Hoggit asked.

Steadfast turned back toward the sergeant, who was standing at attention. "Sergeant Ernesta Stout, Mr. Hoggit, sir."

Hoggit smirked, seemingly to himself, then said, "You have been very useful, Ms. Stout."

"I'm glad I could be of service, sir."

Steadfast was extremely confused. What was Hoggit doing down here? What did he mean about Stout being very useful? Steadfast thought it was time to flex a little bit of his authority.

"What's going on, Reed?" he said sharply. "I'm guessing you know and you owe me an explanation."

Hoggit couldn't hide his sneer, though there was nothing to indicate that he was trying to. "Don't worry yourself about it."

"I think you're forgetting who you're talking to. It's my job to worry myself about it—and it's your job to report to me about it!"

Hoggit rolled his eyes. "If you say so."

Steadfast could feel his blood boiling, and it wasn't from the heat of the factory. "Hoggit, you owe me some answers, and I want them now."

Unbelievably, the COO's only "answer" was to produce a bag of potato chips from his suit pocket. He opened the bag and began to crunch noisily. He didn't seem to notice or care that he was dropping crumbs all over his expensive clothing.

"Hoggit, do I need to remind you that I'm your superior?"

Hoggit's eyes blazed, but only for a second. Then he stuffed another handful of chips into his mouth and spoke while he chomped. "We have a little bit of a situation. Nothing that can't be solved by accessing what's down there."

He shook the last few chips into his mouth, tossed the bag on the floor, and then looked at Stout.

"Guard, take us into the vault," he said.

Steadfast wanted to tell Stout not to take orders from anyone but him, but he realized they had come here to go into the vault, so telling her to stop was pointless.

Stout followed Hoggit's direction, shining the light down the stairs and heading into the vault first. She shined the light back up toward the opening to indicate she had reached the bottom; then the professor started down.

Steadfast turned toward Hoggit, surprised to see that the COO had now produced a bag of hard candies from somewhere and was busy consuming them.

"I'm not going to forget this," Steadfast said.

Hoggit seemed almost bored by Steadfast. "I don't suppose you are." He pointed to the vault door. "After you."

Steadfast was growing increasingly wary. It was as if Hoggit owned the place. Hoggit had seemed so even-keeled during their first meeting; he'd come off as polished and genteel. Maybe it was merely an act and Hoggit didn't see the need to keep it up anymore. Why hadn't Steadfast picked up on it before?

Maybe Hoggit had some plan under way. He had outlasted the recent succession of CEOs—but what did that mean? What strategy did he really have in mind? Or was the professor right, he had a plot of some kind to gain control of the company, or to leave with a hidden treasure?

No doubt, the financial pressures that were obviously plaguing Verity had caused Hoggit to lose his self-control. He certainly had an issue with stress eating.

Once they were past this crisis, Steadfast was going to have to deal with a lot of issues, Hoggit being just one of them. One thing he knew for sure, though, no one was going to act solo. Everyone was going to have to be part of a "we" organization. There was no room for a "me" organization.

Just then, he heard the professor exclaim, "This is amazing!" Steadfast turned away from Hoggit and looked in the opening. When he saw Reposit's excited face staring up at him, he decided to climb down the ladder. What he saw when he got to the bottom was breathtaking. The sight would have lifted his spirits, if it were not for the sound of the hatch door thudding shut; leaving the three of them locked inside.

CHAPTER 8

A Team Is Forged

Even if this current situation is beyond compare
or even comprehension, the only way through a
crisis is together.

—Steadfast

Stout ran up the ladder and threw her weight against the hatch
door. Steadfast wasn't surprised in the least that the door didn't
budge. If what he'd tried to do earlier with the boardroom door
was silly, this was just foolhardy. The closure was a thick slab
of concrete that the sergeant had had trouble moving when it
wasn't latched shut. Both she and the professor yelled for Hoggit
to come back and release them, as though it were even a remote
possibility.

Steadfast scanned the room, though it was difficult to see
much, considering their only source of illumination was Stout's
flashlight. He needed a better idea of where they were, so he took
out his phone again and turned on his flashlight.

What he saw was likely what had amazed the professor. On a
table were a dozen or so intricately rendered glass pieces similar
to the ones he'd seen in the paintings. He ran his light over them
slowly. Even in the midst of their predicament, he couldn't help
marveling at the perfection of the artistry.

He stepped farther into the room and continued searching his surroundings. High up on the back wall, something was glowing. Could it be an emergency light? An exit? He pointed it out to Reposit and Stout, who were still railing at the door.

This seemed to snap them to attention and they stopped. After climbing down the ladder, Stout and Reposit joined Steadfast, and all three of them moved toward the light, their two flashlight beams exploring the terrain. Suddenly Steadfast felt Stout's hand on his shoulder.

"Look there," Stout said, running her light over a tall shelf crammed with papers. "Those must be the stocks and bonds."

If this was indeed an old reserve of stock certificates, they could have enough value to turn Verity's fortunes. The professor got to the shelf first and pulled down a sheet of thick paper. In an instant, Steadfast realized that what Reposit was holding was something else entirely.

"It's just a drawing?" Stout said, clearly disappointed.

The professor held the paper closer to Steadfast's light. "This is hardly *just* a drawing. It's a production design. I've never seen this one before."

Steadfast brought his light closer. The drawing was a fanciful creature, seemingly part bird and part land animal, with layered plumage. It was beautiful and stirred a sense of wonder inside Steadfast that he was unaccustomed to; it seemed completely incongruous in this situation.

Reposit handed the drawing to Steadfast and then pulled several more from the shelves.

"This is remarkable," he said. "I have never seen any of these. These designs either never made it to production or have been lost. In either case, this is a treasure trove."

Stout seemed unmoved by this. She went to the shelves and quickly leafed through the papers. "There are no stocks and bonds here," the sergeant said. "Just...doodles."

Reposit drew in such a sharp breath Steadfast momentarily thought the man was having a heart attack. "Just doodles? Just doodles? Do you have any idea what this could mean? If Verity decided to produce these designs, the world would stand in awe."

It might be difficult to produce anything if we're bankrupt, Steadfast thought, but kept it to himself. Reposit wasn't wrong to be excited by this discovery, but there were practical matters to consider. One was the company's current fortunes, or lack thereof. The other was the fact that, like the drawings, they were locked away in a vault and there was an excellent chance the only other person who knew their whereabouts had no intention of letting them out.

Reposit had found some metal carrying tubes and was starting to roll up the drawings. Meanwhile, Steadfast continued to search for some kind of exit. He ran his beam toward the light he'd seen before—more a glow, really—coming from an elaborate sketch of the crystal cupola. He turned to show it to Stout when he saw her jump back and shout in pain.

"Something just burned me," she said sharply. She shined her flashlight upward, which revealed thick, golden drops coming from cracks in the ceiling. "It's molten glass."

Steadfast and Stout locked eyes, indicating they both knew who was responsible for this. Steadfast looked back to where the molten glass originated and as he did, another drop landed on one of the drawings that had fallen to the floor. The drawing instantly caught fire, and Stout stomped on the paper in an effort to put it out.

The professor hadn't seemed to notice what was happening. "What do you think you're doing? If you can't treat these precious documents with more respect—"

Steadfast cut off his recrimination mid-sentence as another drawing caught fire. And another. Reposit pulled a stack of

drawings from the shelves and moved them away from the growing stream. He went to retrieve more, but within seconds the
entire shelf was on fire and he couldn't reach them in time.

Stout ran up the ladder and started pushing again on the
vault door. Reposit was scrambling to get the drawings he'd saved
into tubes. Meanwhile, the flames grew more intense. Steadfast
guessed they didn't have much time before the entire vault would
be consumed—including them.

"Listen to me," he shouted. "We have to work together—as a
team—if we're going to make it out of here. Even if this current
situation is beyond compare or even comprehension, the only
way through a crisis is together." *That much I know for certain,*
Steadfast reminded himself for a small boost of encouragement.

As he finished saying this, Steadfast noticed a glow coming
from the cup on this belt. He looked down to find the word
COOPERATION shimmering at him. The cup seemed to like this
shift in his approach and he was sure the word would join the
others etched around the surface as an indelible reminder.

However, there was no time to linger on the cup now. They
had to get out, and the vault door was clearly not an option.
As he spun around looking for some other exit, Steadfast saw
something he hadn't noticed before—the drawing of the crystal
cupola, affixed high on the wall, wasn't just glowing, it seemed to
have a tiny bit of light behind it.

He raced over to a rack on the opposite wall and urged the
other two to help him move it under the drawing. As the heat
rose and smoke started to billow, they scrambled up the rack.
When Steadfast got to the top, he pounded his fist against the
drawing—it tore to reveal a dimly lit opening. It was possible the
passage led nowhere, but as Steadfast looked down at the vault in
flames, he was sure it was their only hope.

Shining her flashlight, the sergeant went first and led the

way. The professor, carrying three tubes of drawings, went next. Finally, Steadfast followed, a *whoosh* of flame nearly joining him. The three scrambled through a couple of tight curves and inclines in the cramped stone passage. The smoke, though not enough to make it impossible to breathe, reminded them to move quickly.

Finally, they reached the end of the tunnel, which was covered by a clear glass panel. Without a word, Stout broke the glass, and the three of them carefully stepped through and found themselves standing...where? They were in some kind of fantastic garden, walled off from the factory by a high, ivy-covered chain-link fence.

Getting his breathing under control, Steadfast looked around. What he saw dazzled him. Glass flowers blooming in a rainbow of colors. Glass butterflies and birds—some big, some small, some striped and others spotted—perched in the ivy. Glass cats curled on park benches and, in the center of the garden, a large emerald hummingbird seemed to hover in the air. Around the garden's edges, abstract sculptures stood in graceful groups.

Stout dragged one of the larger abstracts over the passage to block the smoke still drifting out.

"What is this place?" Steadfast said.

Ernesta made a slow three-sixty. "It looks like an old security cage for warehouse valuables."

"Not anymore it isn't," said a soft voice behind them. All three turned at the sound. "Just who are you, and what are you doing in my garden?"

CHAPTER 9

No Looking Back

Second guessing and looking back was not an
option. They had to look ahead and literally
move ahead.

—Steadfast

Steadfast spun around to face a petite Asian woman with salt-
and-pepper cropped hair and perfect bangs making a neat line
across her face. She held a long metal tube in her raised hand.
Steadfast didn't feel threatened by the woman—she seemed
rather frail—but Stout obviously did. In an instant, the sergeant
was standing between him and the woman, in a stance that suggested she was willing to take a bullet for him.

"Whoa," Stout said. "Let's put that thing down now. We don't
want anyone getting hurt."

The professor stepped forward. "It's not a weapon."

"We don't know that."

"We *do* know that," Reposit said, looking at the delicate older
woman. "It's a blowpipe, isn't it? A tool used for glass blowing."

The woman lowered the pipe and shuffled her feet back a step.
"That's right. Not many outsiders know that." Steadfast watched
her eye the three of them carefully. "Who are you?"

Stout took the introductions upon herself. "I'm Sergeant

Ernesta Stout. This is Professor Reposit, and I assume you know that this is the CEO, Mr. Steadfast."

The woman's eyes narrowed. "CEO of what?"

Steadfast chuckled. "Of Verity. At least I was when I woke up this morning."

"I thought the CEO had a different name. Spikes, or something like that."

It took Steadfast a moment to register the name. Leon Spikes wasn't even the *previous* CEO. He'd been gone a couple of years now. "Spikes is no longer with the company."

The woman shrugged. "If you say so."

This seemed to rile Stout. "If you don't know who Mr. Steadfast is, then you're obviously an intruder."

Reposit said, "Well, to be honest, I didn't recognize him right away either, and—"

Stout put up a hand. "Not my point." She turned back to the woman. "Tell us who you are now. I've been working here for a few years and I've never seen you before."

The woman smiled softly, conveying unusual warmth. Suddenly, she didn't seem so frail. She seemed elfin. "My name is Tiffany Tiasang. The reason you haven't seen me is because I'm not really part of the mainstream of Verity. I'm the last designer on staff."

This seemed to catch Reposit's attention. "I've read about you. You're something of a legend. You've been with the company a very long time."

Tiffany nodded. "Nearly forty years."

"You had a chance to work with some of the greats."

Tiffany's voice grew wistful. "Yes, I did. When I started, there were dozens of us in the design department. To be honest, I expected to be fired years ago. I think the only reason they've kept me on is because they forgot I was around."

This made Steadfast feel surprisingly sad. Why was it that the crazier things got around here, the more he wanted to do what he could to make everything right? "Did you make this garden?"

"I did, yes. I have a lot of spare time."

Steadfast walked over to the exquisitely blown hummingbird. Like his cup, the glass bird seemed almost impossibly thin and yet sturdy at the same time. He ran a finger along the hummingbird's throat. Inside the bird's translucent green chest, Tiffany had blown a heart that captured even the modest amount of sunlight coming through the windows above.

He turned back to Tiffany. "This is magnificent. It all is."

"Thank you. I suppose I was born too late. Half a century ago, these designs would be sitting on mantelpieces and in nooks all over the world."

The professor hoisted one of his carry tubes. "You of all people will be fascinated by what I have here." He pulled out some drawings and unrolled them.

Tiffany gasped as she looked through the sketches. "Where did you get these?"

Reposit pointed toward the opening Stout had covered. "From down there."

Tiffany followed his gesture. "What's down there? To tell you the truth, until the three of you came crashing through the window, it never even dawned on me to think about where it might lead."

The sergeant had been quiet for a long time, exploring the garden. Now she spoke up. "It's a secret vault. Though I'm not sure how much of a secret it was, since *I* knew about it and the security staff has been speculating about it for years."

Tiffany stared off in the distance. "Amazing."

Steadfast came closer to her, sweeping widely with his arm. "*This* is amazing. You're an extremely skilled artist, Ms. Tiasang."

Tiffany tilted her head toward him. "Thank you." She pointed to the cup at his belt. "That's one of ours, isn't it?"

Steadfast unlatched the cup and held it out to her. An inch of golden elixir swirled in the bottom. There was definitely more in there now than when they entered the factory. Steadfast realized the level of liquid was definitely rising and falling.

"Yes it is. Do you know anything about this liquid inside of it?"

"I can't say that I do." She ran her fingers over the carved words. "This is unusual."

"You don't know the half of it. They've been etching themselves around the cup one by one: responsibility, curiosity, cooperation."

She looked up at him. "All good things."

"All good things, yes. But like so many other things that have happened today, a bit of a mystery."

Just then, Stout came up to him. "You need to see this."

She brought the group over to the wall that abutted the factory and pointed down. Steadfast's eyes widened as he saw a golden glow seeping through various crevices at an increasing rate. "Is that molten glass?"

"You bet it is," Stout said. "The furnace must be emptying itself everywhere, not just into the vault."

As they watched, the glass pooled on the floor, growing thicker and faster. They had to step back to avoid being incinerated; the pool was following them and spreading. Steadfast realized the entire floor was going to be covered soon. They had to get out of here. Going back the way they came wasn't an option, since the vault was either still burning or a smoke-filled husk at this point, and it was locked on the other side.

"How do you come and go from here?" Steadfast asked Tiffany.

"Through that door."

She pointed in a direction already covered in molten glass.

Stout clambered up onto a table and gestured for the rest of them to do the same.

"My work," Tiffany said solemnly. "It's all going to melt."

Stout took her by the shoulders. "*We're* going to melt if we don't find a way out of here."

Steadfast tried to keep his wits about him, though it was getting tougher as he imagined what would happen when the glass reached them. Second-guessing and looking back was not an option. They had to look—and literally move—ahead.

"We've got to get higher," Steadfast shouted. He looked toward the ivy-covered fence a few feet away. "Can all of you jump from here to there?"

They agreed they could. Then on the count of three, all four of them leaped together and caught on, rattling the length of the fence. Stout quickly climbed up, the others following after her. Steadfast had been concerned about Tiffany, but she surprised him with her strength and nimbleness.

When they got to the top of the fence, they looked down at the factory floor. There was molten glass everywhere, causing everything in its path to burst into flames. Steadfast looked back at the garden. As Tiffany predicted, her gorgeous creations were in the process of returning to their previous form.

"There's no way out," the professor said mournfully.

"Don't think that way," Steadfast said. "We need to work together. We're a team, remember?" He looked at his cup again, eyeing the word COOPERATION. That must have been what added the elixir earlier. "We've even gained a new member. Let's work together. The last time we did that, something extraordinary happened. Maybe if we—"

Steadfast suddenly found himself speechless—which seemed to be the only appropriate response to seeing a large glass hummingbird grow ten times its size, stretch its wings, and ascend above them, its glowing heart beating.

CHAPTER 10

Taking Flight

I believe in my art.

—Designer Tiffany Tiasang

The oversize glass hummingbird rose to meet them where they were hanging near the top of the fence. Steadfast's eyes shifted from the bird's fluttering wings—*how did glass do that?*—to the emerald heart beating inside.

"Oh, my goodness," Tiffany said, her voice filled with wonder.

Steadfast turned to see her pointing down. He looked to find something even more amazing than the bird hovering just a few feet away: Emerging from the molten ooze were Tiffany's pieces, which had been destroyed only minutes before. Cats and unicorns and zebras. Daisies and roses and tulips. Abstracts were twisting and curling as they rose from their grave. All of them were rising up to meet the quartet on the fence. Most kept a certain distance, but a collection of tiny glass butterflies flew within inches of Steadfast, flitting around the cup that he'd reattached to his belt.

Stout reached out a finger toward one of the butterflies, and it darted away from her. The sight of it made Steadfast chuckle. He was hanging on for his life as the heat rose, and no escape was imminent, yet he still found something to laugh about.

Suddenly, Steadfast heard a *whoomph*. He turned toward the factory.

"The shipping cartons have caught fire," the sergeant said. "This is very, very bad."

Steadfast thought it was a fairly accurate assessment. In spite of the remarkable things happening at this very moment in Tiffany's garden, their situation was dire. It seemed possible that the entire factory was going to blow up, with no functional sprinkler system or backup to combat the impending disaster.

Steadfast didn't want to think about what the next minutes were going to be like. He was totally unprepared. It had never entered his mind that as CEO he'd literally be responsible for people's lives.

The other three seemed to understand the ramifications. They were all looking at the factory now, wordlessly. Steadfast turned back toward the garden. *If I'm going to go down*, he thought, *at least I'll go down taking in the remarkable work Tiffany has done. At least I will have experienced Verity at its finest.*

The hummingbird had moved even closer to him, no more than a couple of feet away, and seemed as though it was nodding to him. Following some mysterious instinct, Steadfast reached out a hand toward the glass masterpiece. The bird rested against his hand, and Steadfast felt a deep sense of calm settle into him. They stayed like this for several seconds, which Steadfast wished could last into eternity.

Then the bird pulled back, dipped, and shot up toward the top of the fence. As it did, its tail started to grow into a pliable, rainbow-hued ribbon. Flying in a graceful arc, the bird looped the ribbon around the top of the fence. Then it continued flying toward the catwalk above the factory floor. Steadfast saw that the other pieces were joining the hummingbird, melding into the ribbon, giving it greater substance and width. Finally, the bird landed on the catwalk, turned back toward Steadfast, and melted into the rainbow ribbon.

Steadfast could barely believe his eyes, though his perception of what was possible was changing by the minute. Had he participated in some way by reaching out to the hummingbird?

"I knew they could do it," Tiffany said.

The professor, who had been strangely quiet for a long time, pointed, tracing the path of the ribbon. "Do you think that thing is solid? Is that a way for us to make it over to the catwalk and get out of here?"

Stout spoke up. "Are you kidding? That ribbon is extending straight over the furnace. If we slip on the *glass ribbon*, we're done for."

"Well, if we stay here," Reposit said, "we're definitely done for."

The sergeant glared at him, but she didn't fire back, likely because she realized he was right.

Tiffany seemed to ignore their debate; instead, she moved to the top of the fence and started to climb onto the ribbon.

Steadfast yelled after her. "Tiffany, be careful. It looks very dangerous."

Tiffany dipped her head toward him, instantly reminding Steadfast of the hummingbird. "I believe in my art," she said serenely, after which she turned and stepped on to the ribbon. She did so gingerly, but once she tested it, she turned toward the catwalk. The ribbon was barely wide enough for her to keep both feet on it at the same time, but she made it across, deliberately taking one step at a time. Steadfast noticed that she never once looked down. When she got to the catwalk, she turned back to the others, beaming.

"Let's go," Stout said. Without a backward glance, the sergeant climbed up on the ribbon, tested her weight, and then walked across.

By this point, both the professor and Steadfast had moved

atop the fence. Reposit looked at Steadfast, and he could tell the professor was reluctant.

"This is crazy, isn't it?" Reposit asked.

"It was crazy for them, too."

The professor grinned nervously.

Steadfast put a hand on Reposit's shoulder. "You'll be fine." He nodded toward the metal tubes strapped on Reposit's shoulder and pushed behind his back. "We need to get that precious cargo someplace safe."

This seemed to embolden the professor, and without another word, he climbed up on the ribbon. His bravery lasted about a half-dozen steps, after which his legs seemed to get a little wobbly.

Steadfast called after him. "You're good, professor. The ribbon will hold you."

Reposit took a deep breath and then continued forward. Seconds later, he was across.

Steadfast was the only one left. He looked down at the garden floor, which was now a sea of molten glass. It appeared all of the pieces that were going to come to life had done so already.

His three colleagues on the other side were beckoning to him. Steadfast had watched each make their way across the ribbon of glass with varying degrees of confidence—but they'd all made it. Still, doing so himself gave him pause. He'd always been a little afraid of heights, and if he was going to be honest with himself, he'd always been more than a little cautious about, well, everything.

Caution really wasn't a choice now, though, was it? There were times when you had to take chances instead. The ribbon had worked for the others; he had to believe it was going to work for him as well.

It took him a minute or so to pull himself into position. Touching the glass ribbon, he was startled by how smooth the surface felt. Smooth glass was slick glass. He was wearing brand-new shoes. Would they be too slippery?

Steadfast closed his eyes as he willed himself to move forward. What had Tiffany said before she made the crossing? "I believe in my art." This multicolored ribbon was in many ways the greatest manifestation of Tiffany's artistry. Did Steadfast believe in it as well? He knew there was a reason help had come to them. There was a reason everything was happening. Opening his eyes and gazing across at his colleagues, he knew the ribbon would carry him.

As Steadfast began his passage, he caught a glow in his peripheral vision. He guessed something more had been etched on his cup, but looking at the cup required looking down, and that probably wasn't a good idea. Instead, he kept his eyes fixed on Tiffany, Stout, and the professor, all cheering him forward.

Soon, he was at the catwalk. The sergeant extended a hand to help him on, though he didn't really need it. Steadfast surprised himself by pulling the three others into a group hug as he glanced back toward the ribbon. As he did, the ribbon started to melt, transforming first into rainbow-colored droplets, and then back into the sculptures that had formed it. The butterflies fluttered away. The land animals touched softly onto the ground and scampered off, unaffected by the molten glass and the fires that continued around them. The abstracts re-formed and spiraled out of sight. And finally the hummingbird re-emerged from the liquid. It turned to Steadfast, dipped its head one more time, and flew off.

Now that they were all safe, Steadfast finally looked down at his cup. On it the word TRUST was now visible. Yes, he'd indeed required—and shown—trust in the past few minutes. He wasn't surprised when there was more elixir inside the cup as well.

For the second time in the past few minutes, Steadfast chuckled out of relief and maybe a bit of awe. Then he looked at Stout.

"Lead the way, sergeant."

CHAPTER 11

Back on Track

Perhaps there's magic in our history?
—Designer Tiffany Tiasang

Now that they were high above the factory floor, the quartet of CEO Steadfast, professor Reposit, security guard Stout, and designer Tiffany Tiasang had to get out of there safely, before the smoke rising from the smoldering fires overtook them.

"Where does this catwalk lead?" Steadfast asked, trying to locate an exit.

Stout pointed to a bend in the rigging, around which Steadfast couldn't see. "There's a door over there. Let's get moving."

As if on cue, Steadfast felt a spray of water on his back. Had the power come back on? He could see spray coming from various sprinkler heads. At the very least, some kind of emergency generator had kicked in. It wasn't going to be enough to prevent the factory from needing huge repairs—the damage was past that point—but maybe it would be enough to keep the building from collapsing.

"We have to get out of here," the professor said. "We can't let the drawings get soaked."

The four of them ran across the catwalk in the direction the sergeant had pointed. When they got to the door, it was locked—which seemed to Steadfast to be a considerable safety hazard—but Stout quickly found the right key on the well-equipped ring looped to her belt and opened the door.

Closing the door behind them, they stood in a dark vestibule. The lights still weren't working, which meant not all the power had come back on. They were standing in front of stairs, which Stout, shining her flashlight, said led back up to the mezzanine.

"Back to where we should have gone in the first place," Reposit said.

Steadfast wanted to disagree with him, but he knew the professor was right. Choosing the path that had seemed easier had been a poor decision on his part, something he would remember in the future. He nodded toward Reposit and then began to climb the stairs with Stout in the lead. The others fell in behind him with Reposit, predictably, complaining about his knees.

They reached the door to the portrait gallery and went in. How long had it been since they'd last been here? An hour, maybe two at the most? Yet so much had changed in that time. Steadfast had seen remarkable things—the cache of drawings, Tiffany's spectacular garden, and the beautiful experience with the hummingbird and other pieces. He'd also encountered more danger than he'd ever faced in his life. He'd learned that he—and all of Verity—had an enemy in Reed Hoggit. People talk about enemies at work, but this was different. This felt like the real thing. Steadfast still wasn't sure what Hoggit's agenda was or why that agenda involved locking them all in the vault, but there was no question that Hoggit did not have the best interests of Verity in mind.

Their trial by actual fire, their "quest," as the elevator operator had called it, had provided Steadfast with one more thing: a team. Team-building had always mattered to Steadfast, but in all of his management training classes and all his experience, he'd never gone through a simulation—or an actual crisis—that involved the equivalent of crossing a glass ribbon over a raging fire. He couldn't argue with the effectiveness of it.

In the limited natural light, Steadfast glanced down at his cup. It was now a third full of golden elixir.

As he stood there catching his breath, Steadfast noticed that the sprinkler system had drenched him. His new suit had taken a pounding, but he'd get over that. Looking at the others, he saw that they were also sopping wet.

"We're quite a ragged bunch, aren't we?" he asked.

Stout drew herself to attention. "I'm feeling quite strong, sir."

Steadfast smiled at her kindly. "I'm sure you are, Ernesta."

They walked along the hall of the portrait gallery until they reached the opening where the painting of Crystal Modello had been. As before, Steadfast took out his phone and shined the light up into the dark tunnel. Then he turned toward Reposit.

"Do you really think this is the Worthy Way?"

"I'm convinced of it."

Steadfast nodded slowly. "You said this particular part was called the Perilous Passage?"

"That's what the legends call it."

"Probably can't be much more perilous than the passages we've already been on, huh?"

The professor seemed terrified at the thought. "I certainly hope not."

Stout pulled out her truncheon, as though it would be useful in dealing with any dangers they might encounter. "I'll walk point, sir."

Steadfast was again tempted to salute, but he just smiled instead. "That might be wise."

The sergeant nodded sharply. "Should we get going?"

Steadfast moved to do so, but he stopped when Tiffany tapped his shoulder. "There's something you should know about."

"What's that?"

"There's a storeroom. I might be the only person in the company who still knows about it. It houses a sample of each of our artisan creations like the ones in some of these paintings."

"I've never heard about such a storeroom," Reposit said.

Tiffany simply looked at him, and the professor's shoulders slumped. Steadfast realized this had been a humbling day for the company's historian.

Tiffany continued. "Years ago, when Verity stopped making fine art and started concentrating on bottles, the board decided they were going to auction off all of these pieces. But the night before the auction, our head designer secreted them away to this storeroom. Only the head designers who followed have known about the location. I was never actually named head designer— for years I've been the *only* designer, so I guess it goes without saying that I'm also the head—but the last one told me the location before she left. I've never actually gone to the storeroom. I was afraid it would be too sad for me."

Steadfast smiled softly at Tiffany. "That's fascinating, but I'm not sure we can deal with that right now."

"You saw what happened with the hummingbird and the other pieces in my garden, right?"

"It was difficult to miss."

"What if there's magic in all of these artisan pieces? Perhaps there's magic in our history."

Steadfast's mind swam at the notion. Tiffany's designs had saved them. The cup on his belt was clearly something other than a normal cup. Was it possible that all the works of art had—Steadfast couldn't believe he was thinking this—*magical* properties? That the true power of the company resided in these creations?

"What you're saying is absolutely worth exploring, but I can't take us off of our path again. I've done that once already, and it was nearly catastrophic."

Tiffany met his eyes. "I understand that. I'm not asking you to veer from your path. You have a quest to reach the crystal cupola and find the Treasure Beyond All Price. But I think my quest is to find out if those items are in the storeroom. Maybe they can help."

"I don't love the idea of your going off on your own. There are dangers out there. I haven't even told you about what Reed Hoggit did to us."

"Hoggit is a pig," Tiffany said with surprising bitterness. Steadfast guessed that there was some history Tiffany wasn't mentioning. "Don't worry about me. I'm tougher than I look."

Steadfast acknowledged that she'd already proven this to be true. "You need to be very careful."

"I will be."

Then she pointed to the tubes Reposit was carrying. "Those might be better off coming with me. If nothing else, I can lock them away in the storeroom."

Reposit's only response was to clutch the tubes to his chest.

"Think about it, professor," Steadfast said. "It's unlikely this thing is called the Perilous Passage because it's a walk in the park."

For several seconds, Reposit did nothing. Then he begrudgingly held the tubes out to Tiffany. "Everything is still dry inside. I checked."

Tiffany took the tubes. "Good work."

Without further comment, she turned and headed the other direction. Steadfast, Stout, and even Reposit wished her well.

When Tiffany disappeared from view, Steadfast turned to look at the others. "Are you all ready to follow the Worthy Way?"

"I certainly am," the professor said.

The sergeant didn't say anything. She simply drew herself up into the dark passage and gestured for them to follow.

CHAPTER 12

Perilous Indeed

If they maintained the values of responsibility,
curiosity, cooperation, and trust, they would find
their way out of this impossible challenge.

—Steadfast

The steady climb up rung after rung of the Perilous Passage was both tedious and exhausting, though it didn't seem to be particularly perilous. Yes, falling down the passage would be dangerous, maybe even fatal, but there were handholds everywhere. Steadfast found himself climbing in a rhythm, his legs and arms in sync with Stout's. Reposit appeared to be holding his own, though he seemed to be using more energy complaining about the effort than in exerting it.

The cup at Steadfast's belt provided new assistance now. The glowing elixir served to light the immediate surroundings, easing their passage. Steadfast wondered about the extraordinary gift Nora had given him. Did she even realize how magical it was? Had someone special given it to her? He was going to have to find out—but how would he even broach the topic, given how preposterous it would all sound? One thing he knew for sure, though: The cup was sending a clear message to him. He knew if they maintained the values of responsibility, curiosity, cooperation, and trust, they would find their way out of this impossible challenge.

Steadfast had been so lost in thought he didn't notice Stout had stopped climbing and turned on her flashlight.

"Problem, Ernesta?"

"I don't think so. We've come to the end of the passage and there's a panel in the ceiling. I think I can…" She grunted as she shoved at the panel. "Got it."

Light streamed through the opening, as did something else—a stench unlike anything Steadfast had smelled since his best friend's college dorm room.

"What is that?" the professor said behind him, the disgust evident in his voice.

Stout coughed. "It's really awful." She climbed up and reported, "We're in an office. At least I think that's what this is."

Though his nose protested, Steadfast followed her into the room. It did indeed seem to be an office, a large and elegant one at that. Steadfast had half expected to find a dead body, but the stench seemed to be coming from the debris.

He watched Reposit step gingerly through the mess. "I can't believe someone would treat such a nice place with such disrespect." Suddenly, he moved toward a couch that was groaning under piles of books and papers. He pulled a volume from the awkward stack, causing several to tumble to the carpet. "Wait a second. I know this book. I loaned it to—"

"Me, I believe," came a voice behind them. "You loaned it to *me*."

Steadfast pivoted to see Reed Hoggit. The COO appeared to have put on twenty pounds since they had last seen him outside the vault. His shirt was straining at its buttons and his beard was unkempt, animal-like. Even his nose seemed fatter. Steadfast was momentarily flummoxed at the sight of the man, but he quickly recovered.

"I don't even know where to begin with you, Hoggit. Your behavior at the vault was beyond unacceptable—it was criminal. I'm suspending you without pay immediately.

Hoggit slowly turned in Steadfast's direction, exuding boredom and derision. "Please, Steadfast. Do you really think you can *discipline* me?"

"You report to me, Hoggit. I order you off the premises immediately."

Hoggit scoffed. "Look at the big CEO throwing his weight around. Really, Steadfast, you're adorable."

Reposit walked between them, holding various books. "These texts—I loaned you all of these."

"That you did, Reposit. They've been very useful in my... efforts."

"You used me," Reposit said. "You used my love of the company."

Steadfast was incensed. "What's your game, Hoggit? Whatever it is, we aren't going to let you get away with it."

When the COO looked back at Steadfast, his eyes were cold. "I'm already getting away with it, and I have been for some time. Don't they say that a great leader always makes the most of his resources? I need just a little more—say, the Treasure Beyond All Price—and I'll have everything. And no one will be the wiser once we reopen for business. I'll be seen as the savior after all."

"You're going to have to go through us," Stout said.

Hoggit shrugged and gave her a cursory glance. "To be honest, I thought I already *had* gone through you. I hadn't counted on your getting out of that vault. If we had more time, I'd ask you to explain how you did that. But we don't."

Hoggit's face grew harder and then he made a lunge toward Steadfast. Steadfast instinctively stepped back. This seemed to throw off the COO and he stumbled, but before he could gather himself, he slipped on a sloppy takeout carton. With all his momentum thrusting him forward, Hoggit banged his head on the coffee table and landed with a thud.

Stout moved to stand over him.

"He's not dead, is he?" Steadfast said.

"We wouldn't be that lucky. I can see him breathing. Let's get out of here before he wakes up."

Just then, there was a knock on the window. Steadfast turned toward it.

"Come out to the balcony." It was a window washer sitting on his rig. He must have been observing the whole scene. "I can help you get away," he shouted.

Steadfast wasn't sure there was a point to it. "Thanks, but we can just go out the office door."

Right after he said it, though, he noticed Hoggit stirring. The three of them could probably make it to the door before the COO came to his senses, but they were closer to the balcony. They ran toward it, and as Hoggit drew himself up to his knees, the three of them stepped onto the window washer's lift.

As the window washer began to lower his rig to take them down, Steadfast looked through the office window and saw Hoggit's incensed eyes staring back at him.

CHAPTER 13

Downs and Ups

Every time I clean a window, I make the world a
little clearer.

—Joe the window washer

The window washer lowered them slowly, which was just fine with Steadfast; his adventure on the glass ribbon had done less to cure him of his fear of heights than he might have liked. When they were two stories below Hoggit's thirteenth-floor office, the window washer pulled the stop lever.

"We'll be okay here while you figure out what you want to do next," he said and extended his hand. Steadfast shook it. "I'm Joe Wischer."

"Nice to meet you, Joe. I'm Vince Steadfast."

"Nice to meet you, too. What do you do at Verity?"

"I'm the new CEO."

This information seemed to surprise Joe. He peered up toward Hoggit's office. "Looks like that guy wants your job."

Steadfast grimaced. "He definitely wants something. Or maybe he just wants everything."

Reposit jumped into the conversation and started explaining to Joe all that had happened on their quest so far. Steadfast was happy to let the professor take over, because he needed a minute or two to gather himself and to try to assess the situation. The company might actually be on the verge of bankruptcy. The entire staff had been sent home unsure if they had jobs any longer. The factory had suffered major damage. Strange, fantastical things had been happening. Oh, yes, and a psychopath had already tried to seriously hurt him and his colleagues twice this morning.

Reposit had pulled out *A Brief Compendium* and was showing Joe something about Crystal Modello when Steadfast interrupted.

"I think we need to assess what we're doing here," he said.

It must have been the way he said it, because everyone stopped talking and looked at him, including the professor, who was mid-lecture. Now that their eyes were on him, Steadfast felt less certain about how to continue, but he did so anyway.

"We're currently pretty much hanging by a thread on the side of Verity Tower. That's not why any of us got out of bed this morning, and it is much more than any company should ever ask of you."

Stout stiffened when he said this, but Steadfast didn't want to stop.

"We have no idea if this Treasure Beyond All Price actually exists—"

The professor interrupted. "Well, I—"

Steadfast held up a finger to stop the professor. "And even if it does, we have no idea if it can actually help Verity out of its current situation. Then there's the fact that the treasure itself is rumored to be dangerous and, whether it is or not, we know Hoggit is *definitely* dangerous. I'm starting to believe it doesn't make sense to continue to take such a huge risk with no end in sight."

For a moment, no one spoke. Then Stout broke the silence. "Certainly from a risk assessment standpoint, you're right, sir."

Reposit closed *A Brief Compendium* and put it back in his satchel. "And the rumors do speak of danger."

Steadfast studied them for a second and then said to Joe, "We need to do the sensible thing here and regroup down below, outside the building. We can consider the quest at some later point, but our safety comes first. Can you take us to the ground?"

Joe offered a thoughtful expression Steadfast couldn't completely interpret. Finally, he pointed to the cup at Steadfast's belt.

"That's an awfully nice cup you have there. Think I could take a closer look?"

Steadfast thought it was a curious time to be asking such a thing, but he really had no reason to deny the request. He unstrapped the cup, noticing as he did that nearly all of the elixir was gone. *Okay, I get it, you don't approve,* he said in his mind to whoever or whatever was filling and draining his cup. *I'm still going to do the practical thing here.*

He handed the cup to Joe, who turned it admiringly and then pinged it. The sound was as clear and long as it had been in the elevator this morning, seeming to fill the air around them even though they were outside.

"Yeah, this is a beauty," Joe said. "You know, I come from a long line of glass artists who worked here at Verity."

Steadfast hadn't anticipated this. "Really?"

"Yup. My family made everything—sculptures, fine glasswork." He pointed to the top of the building and Steadfast looked up, even though he couldn't see very far from this angle. "That thing up there."

That caught the professor's attention. "You're saying your family created the crystal cupola?"

"A bunch of generations ago, yeah. My great-great-grandfather or something like that, on my mother's side. Several members of the Kunstler line worked here."

Reposit's jaw actually dropped. "Your great-great-grandfather was Dieter Kunstler?" the professor said.

"That was him," Joe replied.

"He was a genius, an artist with a capital A."

"So I've heard. I'm afraid I didn't inherit any of his talent for making things out of glass." He picked up his squeegee. "I'll bet I'm a whole lot better at cleaning it than he ever was, though. Based on how this place looks, they could use a lot more of my services."

Steadfast noticed there was no irony in Joe's tone when he said it. He took real pride in his ability to excel at his work.

Joe handed the cup back to Steadfast. "Anyway, that's an awfully special thing you have there."

"Yes, it is."

As Steadfast refastened the cup on his belt, he thought about Nora and about the warmth that had filled her note. How was he going to tell her that her faith in him was unwarranted, that when tested on his first day he'd failed so badly he'd in essence turned the company over to a madman? Maybe he should just give the cup to Joe. The window washer seemed more deserving of it.

Joe dipped his squeegee in his bucket and then used it on the corner of the window in front of them. "I have a saying: 'Every time I clean a window, I make the world a little clearer.'"

Steadfast smiled at him. "That's a lovely philosophy."

"I like to think so." He held the squeegee out to Steadfast. "Why don't you give it a try?"

The suggestion caught Steadfast by surprise. He wasn't entirely "allergic" to cleaning, as his wife claimed, but he probably hadn't touched a squeegee in a couple of decades. Still, Joe had made window washing sound romantic, so Steadfast took the proffered handle. He followed the line Joe had started, which was surprisingly grimy. Verity Tower gleamed from a distance, but it wasn't nearly as shiny up close. It took a few passes with the squeegee to wash away the dirt. As he did, Steadfast noticed something etched in the glass.

"Hey, look at this," he said to the others, pointing to the image of the crystal cupola.

Reposit moved close to the imprint. "The Sign of the Shining Cupola."

Stout leaned in. "This is definitely a sign."

Steadfast wasn't sure what either of them were talking about, especially Ernesta, who didn't seem terribly interested in things like signs. "What are you getting at?"

The sergeant drew herself up. "It's a sign that the quest needs to continue."

Steadfast's impatience was overtaking him. He pointed to the etching. "You got that from looking at *this*?"

Reposit reached in his bag and retrieved *A Brief Compendium* and recited from it. "'The Sign of the Shining Cupola may mark an alternative entrance to the Worthy Way and lead to—'" He looked up at the others. "'—the Treasure Beyond All Price.'"

Steadfast's first thought was to scoff. He got over it in a split second, though. Could he mock any suggestion of magic at this point? "Do you really think this is a sign?"

Reposit closed his book. "It is most definitely."

Stout nodded sharply. "I'm with the professor on this one."

Steadfast grinned when he saw Reposit's stunned reaction to Ernesta agreeing with him about something. He turned to the window washer. "What do you think, Joe?"

Joe glanced at the window and then at Steadfast. "I think there's a reason we stopped here."

Steadfast closed his eyes and tried to summon what was in his heart. Just a few minutes ago, giving up the quest seemed like such a sensible thing to do. They'd be safer that way. But they wouldn't be better off, would they? And without question the company would be poorer for it.

"We're going to keep this going, aren't we?"

With that, Joe pulled the lever to raise the rig. Steadfast's three companions cheered their assent, which was a sound that warmed his soul. The quest was the right and true thing to do.

If he needed any further confirmation, the cup on his belt provided it. At that very moment it glowed with another word—TRUTH. When Steadfast looked into the cup, he saw that all of the lost elixir had returned, and then some. It was confirmation that he was wise to overcome his fears and focus on the truth. He'd been honest with his team. He'd laid out the risks. And then together they'd move forward with a shared sense of purpose.

It was at this point Steadfast realized he was still holding the squeegee. He handed it to Joe. "You will join us, won't you?"

Joe wrinkled his nose. "I'm not sure I'm quest material."

Steadfast pointed to the window. "You stopped right here. I'd say that makes you *prime* quest material."

"I don't know, I—"

Before Joe could finish speaking, they heard a door slam above them. They all tilted their heads to look up. Steadfast could barely believe what he was seeing. Hoggit was leering down at them—except he was only partially Hoggit now. His nose had grown into a pig snout and there were tusks protruding from his lower jaw. He made an ominous sight.

Things went from frightening to terrifying when Hoggit started to use his tusks to saw at the cables holding the window-washing scaffold.

"We have to get out of here," Steadfast said, unsure of where they could possibly go. Nearly twelve stories up, they were far too high to jump, and he was sure the exterior windows were the unbreakable type that made modern buildings safer. No chance of breaking through.

Steadfast looked down and noticed the elixir in his cup was glowing even more than usual, and as he watched it, he saw a golden mist rise up from the cup toward the window, where it danced around the etching of the crystal cupola. There was a flash and Steadfast inched back. When the flash cleared, the window in front of them was gone.

Steadfast jumped through the window and then turned and reached out a hand to help the others back into the building. Joe was the last to enter. Whatever reluctance he'd had about joining the quest was no longer relevant.

As the window washer stepped in, all four of them turned back to the scaffold—just in time to see it plummet to the street below.

CHAPTER 14

The Red Room

We need you, and you're stronger than you
realize.

—Sergeant Stout

They found themselves in another lavishly appointed conference room. It was a study in red: red leather couches, red drapes, red velvet wing-backed chairs on red carpet. On the center table, chocolate donuts with red icing towered on a tray. On a wet bar beside the fireplace, silver platters displayed strawberries and raspberries. *How many fancy conference rooms does one company need?*

The group seemed mesmerized by the trappings but Steadfast found the entire room off-putting. More wasted expense for a fancy show of opulence. But at least they could eat something before they ventured further into the unknown.

Just then, one of the tall chairs swiveled, revealing a young man with long fashionable dreadlocks and arty red glasses. He was tapping a message on his cell phone, which was somehow projecting red laser beam words in the air all around him. The man didn't seem at all surprised to find four people entering the room from a window eleven stories off the ground.

"Just finishing your latest update," he said. "I'll be with you in one second."

Steadfast found this surprising. "*Our* latest update?"

"Yeah, I've been charting your status since you entered the building. Our followers definitely want to know everything that's happening with the new CEO. Of course, they probably didn't expect what I've been sending them today. Keep this up and you're going to be trending."

"I'm sorry; who are you exactly?"

The man was about to answer when he was distracted by an incoming message. Thumbs flying, he responded rapidly, the red laser beams practically encasing him.

Stout walked up to Steadfast. "His name is Miles Loop. He runs social media for Verity." Stout seemed to study Miles, who was still typing, and then raised her voice. "Why are you still working if the company has been closed down for the day?"

Miles finished what he was doing and then regarded the sergeant. "We all know how important my job is to Verity and how important transparency is to a company today. A promotion—several in quick succession, actually—is inevitable."

Steadfast wasn't sure if any promotions were inevitable at this point. He assumed Miles's name was on one of the pink slips that had inundated the lobby. How many times had the social media maven posted about those today?

Steadfast was wondering how Loop was tracking them to provide updates when something else dawned on him. "Wait a minute; your phone is working. Nobody else can get a signal. Why is that?"

"I have the best phone coverage money can buy. Mr. Hoggit made sure of it."

At the mention of Hoggit, Steadfast's blood pressure rose. He warned himself, *Be very careful with this man.*

"Where are you headed next?" Loop asked. "Our followers want to know."

"Where the four of us are headed is not something we're willing to share with *followers* right now."

Steadfast waited as Loop typed some more and then looked at him through his laser web. "That's disappointing." He typed one more thing and then powered down his phone. The laser lights extinguished. "I'm ready."

"Ready for what?"

"To join you, of course."

Stout took a step forward. "No one invited you." Steadfast noted an ominous tone in her voice. Was she also wary of this man and his agenda?

"Oh, I'm genuinely hurt," Loop said, standing. "I went offline and everything."

Steadfast wasn't sure what to make of this guy. He didn't like the reference to Hoggit, but Loop suddenly seemed less dangerous as he sat back down and picked up his phone again. He uttered an "um" and held the still-dormant phone out to the others.

There, on the darkened screen, was the Sign of the Shining Cupola—the same one that had been etched on the window that no longer existed—along with the number forty-eight.

"It wants us to go to the forty-eighth floor," Reposit said. "Right near the top of the tower."

Steadfast wasn't sure who "it" was, but he presumed the professor was right.

"I guess we head to the stairs, then."

Reposit groaned. "My knees are never going to survive this."

Stout punched him on the arm. "Come on, prof. We need you and you're stronger than you realize."

With that, she moved toward the door, Joe right behind her, and Reposit trailing a few steps back.

Steadfast turned to Loop. "You really want to come with us?"

Loop nodded. "I think you might say I've been with you all along."

Steadfast didn't like the sound of that. He had an uneasy feeling about everything associated with Miles Loop.

On the other hand, maybe it was better to keep this guy close. "Let's go, then."

CHAPTER 15

The Long Climb

We need to give one another a reason to believe
we can all be part of something remarkable, that
together we can make something important
happen.

—Steadfast

They climbed the first few flights uneventfully. Everyone seemed
to be in very good physical shape, except for Reposit, whom he'd
have to watch out for. If they were going to climb all the way to
the forty-eighth floor, the professor was going to require superhu-
man levels of inspiration. Steadfast considered sending him back,
but he knew there was no way the professor would be willing to
leave the quest and all his research behind.

Ten floors up, Joe went on a run to get everyone bottled water
from a break room while the others rested. Steadfast figured this
was a good time to take everyone's temperature.

"Feeling okay, Miles?" he said.

"Walking up stairs is nothing compared to mountain biking."

Steadfast raised his eyebrows. "You bike?"

"Whenever I can." He held up his cell phone. "This stuff'll kill
you if you don't get out into the world, too."

"Good point. Ernesta?"

"Haven't even broken a sweat, sir."

Steadfast grinned. "Maybe once we're finished with this quest you can give me some training tips."

"It would be an honor, Mr. Steadfast."

Finished with the preliminaries, Steadfast turned to Reposit. "Professor? Everything going okay?"

Reposit smiled wanly. "Never been better. No, wait a second, I can think of about eight hundred thousand times I've been better than this."

"You're hanging on, though, right?"

"So far."

Joe returned with the water and a few minutes later they continued the climb. Everyone progressed smoothly for another eight flights. Then, without warning, Reposit dropped to his knees.

"Are my legs still attached to my body? I can't feel them."

Steadfast sat on the step next to the professor. "We can take another rest if you need it."

Reposit grimaced. "What floor are we on?"

Steadfast shined his phone light at the sign on the wall. "We're on twenty-nine."

"Twenty-nine! I thought we were at least in the high thirties by now."

Reposit's body slumped, looking utterly immobile. Steadfast got the sense that if he tried to lift the professor right now—not that it was an option—it would feel like lifting a Reposit-sized sack of sand.

Steadfast considered the alternatives. They could leave Reposit on the stairs, but that could mean exposing the professor to some serious risks. After all, Hoggit—or whatever Hoggit was in the process of becoming—was out there somewhere. They could sit here until Reposit felt like moving on again, but that could be hours from now. He could send a crew, maybe Ernesta and Joe, to the forty-eighth floor, but Steadfast believed he needed to be there to contend with whatever was waiting for them. He realized this required another approach.

He leaned a bit closer to the professor. "Tell me the most extraordinary thing you've discovered in all of your research about Verity."

Reposit looked off in the distance; for a moment Steadfast wasn't certain that the professor had registered his question. Then Reposit looked at Steadfast and his eyes grew clearer

"Do you know what Crystal Modello claimed was her proudest moment?"

"There are a lot to choose from."

"There certainly are. But according to several interviews, it came the morning of Verity's fifth anniversary. The company was a huge success by then, and there was a big gala planned for that evening. But that morning, she was called down to the factory floor. She was worried something had gone wrong and maybe someone had even gotten hurt. When she got there, though, the factory staff presented her with a beautiful hand-blown starburst with a tiny placard that simply read, 'Thanks, Boss.' She kept that in her office until she retired, and her great-great-granddaughter still displays it prominently in her home today."

Steadfast took a moment to absorb this before speaking again. "She created an amazing culture, didn't she?"

"The best."

"We can have that again, you know."

Reposit locked eyes with Steadfast. "Do you really think so?"

"I know we can. We have people like you helping to point the way."

Reposit reached for his bag. "Maybe we could give a copy of *A Brief Compendium* to every employee."

"That's something to consider."

He held the bag closer to his chest. "It wouldn't have to be leather-bound. Doing that would be a little expensive, after all."

"Yes, it would be."

Steadfast watched Reposit gaze into the distance again, and he was concerned that Reposit might be giving up. Then the professor took a deep breath and let it out slowly. "Do you really think it's possible to bring us back to our proudest days?"

"There's no question that it's possible. I think you know this in your heart."

Reposit took another deep breath and then let out a sigh. "I guess I have to get off the stairs if we're going to do that."

"It would help."

Reposit rose slowly, rubbing his right knee for a moment and then standing up straight. "Then let's go."

"Are you sure?"

The professor nodded. "We have a mission to accomplish."

They began to climb again, and as they did Steadfast noticed a glow coming from his cup. He looked down to see the word HOPE shimmering at him. What better sign of hope could there be than seeing the professor now leading the group up the stairs? It was a reminder—not that it was necessary—that each person needed a reason to believe they were part of something remarkable, that together they could make important things happen.

Reposit was going to be awfully sore in the morning. But right now he seemed to be floating on air.

CHAPTER 16

Electronic Madness

If nothing else, the participation in the quest had
given them valuable new dimensions.

—Steadfast

The remaining floors seemed to go by faster, likely because
Steadfast felt as energized by his conversation with Reposit as the
professor himself seemed to be. He knew the professor had to find
a personal reason to carry him forward, but he hadn't expected
Reposit to take to it so quickly. It was gratifying to see. Maybe
every organization, team, and person needed a quest. Maybe the
Worthy Way wasn't so magical or mystical after all.

They exited the stairwell at the forty-eighth floor, but what
now? They had come to this spot, after all, based solely on a sign
from Loop's dormant phone.

"Most of this floor is taken up by the communications center,"
Stout said. She pointed down the hall. "We enter this way."

They reached the door of the communications center a few
moments later. Right there, etched on the door, was the glowing
Sign of the Shining Cupola.

Reposit moved closer to the door to examine it. "I've never
seen this here before. We are *definitely* meant to be here."

Without another word, Stout opened the door and they
entered. The room was a techie's daydream. Huge flat-screen

monitors covered one wall. Banks of computers and all kinds of other electronic equipment filled the rest of the space. It all looked very expensive and very new. No belt tightening here, either.

Of course, everything was lifeless because there seemed to be only limited emergency power in the building. Steadfast remembered Reposit's comment about the ephemeral nature of high technology. The room was like a museum, and they all studied it with their eyes. Except Loop, who had wandered toward a distant corner.

Loop had been true to his word, keeping his own communication device off during their climb, but now he reached into his pocket, pulled out his phone, and hit the power button. Within seconds, red laser beams ignited in every direction until they surrounded the social media wiz.

Steadfast turned nearly as red as the laser light itself when he read the laser beam message:

There is no treasure.
The new CEO is out of his league.
Verity Glassworks is in serious trouble.

Steadfast moved toward Loop to confront him.

"When did you write these messages?"

"I didn't...I don't—"

"Turn that thing off immediately."

"I would, but—"

A new stream of messages burst forth, each more brilliantly lit than the last:

A Treasure Beyond All Price? What a joke!
Get your résumés ready, everyone.
Hoggit is our only hope.

Stout strode past Steadfast and grabbed for the phone. When she did, though, her hand was singed by one of the laser messages, and she leaped backward, blowing on her wound. She pulled out her truncheon and began to approach Loop, who looked terrified in spite of his social media armor.

It's possible that the sergeant would have charged through the lasers to protect Steadfast and the rest of them from Loop's dangerous antics, but that didn't happen, because just then the power suddenly came on. Steadfast felt physically accosted by the bright, dramatic change in the lighting. Meanwhile, the room exploded in a cacophony of noise. Computers booted up, printers issued documents, the television screens broadcast a dozen different images at once—and on top of it all, there was a hum from the huge cooling fan installed in the twenty-foot-tall ceiling.

All of a sudden the television images resolved into a single massive projection. It was Hoggit, looking very well put together and not at all like the piggish manifestation that had leered at them from his office window.

"All of this was meant to remain confidential while we worked on our solutions," he told an interviewer. "Yes, Verity has hit a rough patch, but I promise to restore the business completely—and I'll do it all by myself if I have to."

"Do you think he means it?" Joe asked.

Stout scoffed. "This guy just cut the cables to our lift. Would you trust *anything* he has to say?"

Steadfast was proud of Ernesta. She was still deferential, but twice now she had spoken out and followed her own sense of the right thing to do. If nothing else, her participation in the quest had given her—and maybe all of them—valuable new dimensions.

The interviewer's face was on the screen now. "Well, I assume you'll get some help from your new CEO, Vince Steadfast."

The camera switched back to Hoggit, who chuckled softly.

"I'm afraid I'm not counting on getting much help from Steadfast. To be honest, the board was very divided on him. In my opinion, he's not CEO material."

Steadfast felt everyone's eyes on him. He hoped he wasn't letting the others see it, but Hoggit's comment struck him hard, even considering the source. He had had his very own doubts during the interview process and now, to hear this, on the strangest of all first days. Hoggit was a psycho—but what if he was also right?

"I've seen enough of this," Reposit said. "I say we change the channel."

Steadfast saw Joe look around for some way to turn off the televisions, but the interviewer was back on the screen now.

"What can you tell me about the rumored Treasure Beyond All Price?"

Hoggit laughed as though the interviewer were asking him to confirm the sighting of a yeti. "I can assure you that no such treasure exists."

Reposit yelled at the screen. "What are you saying? You even asked me—"

At that moment, Hoggit—at least the Hoggit on the screen—stopped being their most pressing problem. The cooling fan had blown off its cover, picked up massive speed, and was sucking up loose papers, shredding them on contact. A few seconds later, heavier items like pens and staplers were being pulled into the fan to meet their demise. Even the chairs started shaking and rising toward the ceiling.

Nothing was safe. The fan even tore away the satchel that had been around Reposit's shoulders. The professor screamed, "My life's work!" and managed to grab hold of the strap, but even with his weight behind it, the satchel—and Reposit—inched higher toward destruction.

Steadfast rushed over to grab the professor. "Someone find a way to turn this fan off!"

Stout ran toward the back of the room, calling to Joe. "We need to find the fuse box."

Joe headed toward Stout while Steadfast held his grip on the professor to the degree that he was able.

"Let go of the satchel, professor," Steadfast said. "We might be able to run to safety."

"I'm not letting go. My *Compendium* means everything to me."

"Does it mean enough to die for?"

Steadfast didn't get an answer, because just then the fan stopped and they crashed to the floor. Steadfast sat up, looking around. Reposit must have hit his head, because he seemed dazed. At least he was in one piece, though. Stout came over to help him.

Steadfast slumped against a file cabinet, trying to get his breathing back to normal. He looked across the room to find Loop typing updates into his phone. Why couldn't *that thing* have been caught up in the fan?

Then he glanced up at the television screen. Hoggit was still being interviewed.

"I don't know any other way to say it. Steadfast simply doesn't have what it takes to be a real leader."

In his worry, Steadfast couldn't disagree. *He's right*, Steadfast thought. *All I've done is bring my team into greater and greater danger. That's not leadership; it's recklessness.* Steadfast looked down at his cup and noticed most of the liquid was gone again. He didn't need to wonder where it went, and he wasn't about to kid himself into believing the fan had sucked it up.

Steadfast felt as drained as his cup. All he could think about was his ineffectualness and, truth be told, his stupidity. How could he have been so dumb that he missed all the signs something was seriously wrong at Verity? And more, how could he have thought it would be easy for him to fix whatever had led to the demise of the previous CEOs?

He stood slowly and walked over to Stout, who was still kneeling over the professor, and put a hand on her shoulder. "Is he going to be okay?"

"I think so. Yeah, of course he'll be."

"I'm going to go."

"Go?"

Steadfast didn't answer. He just opened the door of the communications center and left.

❧

CHAPTER 17

A New Dawn

> Once, my mama said if I made a mistake, I should
> say I'm sorry to that person. And then I should
> say sorry to me, too.
>
> —Dawn, the young orphan

His head low, Steadfast walked through the hallway on the forty-eighth floor, contemplating the sorry state of his brief tenure as CEO. He'd promised the employees outside he'd get information for them, and he'd failed. He'd committed to a quest for the Treasure Beyond All Price and then took the easy way out at the first opportunity. He then *recommitted* to the quest and rewarded those who chose to follow him by putting them in harm's way in the communications center. It was becoming more and more likely this would be Steadfast's only day as CEO of Verity. The trials the company was facing were great and, clearly, he wasn't the person who could figure out how to move forward. Maybe the quest had value, but someone else had to lead it.

The question was what to do now. The power was back on, so that probably meant the elevators were working. Maybe he should take one down to the lobby and figure a way out of the building. But before he tried that option, he passed another large conference room and decided to sit for a while. He certainly was in no shape to go home and face his wife. The room, with the shades drawn and the lights off, was nearly as dark as his mood.

Steadfast's cup banged against an armrest when he sat. Once again, he removed it from his belt to examine it, tracing his fingers along the accumulated words: RESPONSIBILITY, CURIOSITY, COOPERATION, TRUST, TRUTH, HOPE. As he'd noticed in the communications center, there were only a few drops of elixir left, though they still managed to cast a glow when he held the cup up to the limited light.

"That's a pretty cup."

Startled, Steadfast nearly jumped from his seat as he turned toward the sound of the young voice. From the shadows in the corner of the room, a girl, who couldn't have been much more than six or seven, stepped forward. Steadfast noticed her headband, which was topped with a white rose.

"Who are you?" he asked softly.

"I'm Dawn."

"I'm Steadfast. It's a little surprising to find you here in this dark conference room."

"I live here."

Steadfast's eyes widened. "You live in this conference room?"

The girl glanced around. "Not here *exactly*. I meant here in this building."

Steadfast didn't know what to make of this. "I'm a little confused, Dawn."

"Mostly, I hide while people are around. Then at night, I have a sleeping place and I sneak out to find food and the stuff I need."

This was difficult to believe, but she was so sincere and the situation was so unusual that he found himself trusting her. Everything else that day had seemed unbelievable yet was turning out to be true. "Do you know how long you've been here? People must be worried about you."

"Not that long, but I'm a good hider."

"You certainly must be. Why do you want to live here, though?"

"It's much better than my foster home." She hesitated, and Steadfast could see the mention of the home was distressing. "I ran away one day and I saw this pretty building with the beautiful thing on top."

"The crystal cupola."

"I guess. So I decided to go inside. It felt like I was in a fairy tale. I loved the giant glass staircase and the big open part in the middle that went up and up."

"The atrium."

"I don't know what that means, but I guess so. Anyway, I've been here ever since. You're not going to make me go back, are you?"

Steadfast couldn't very well allow a little girl to camp out here indefinitely. There had to be a better place for her. "Let's not worry about that for now; I'm not going to do anything to hurt you."

She walked closer to him and touched his hand. "I believe you."

Dawn obviously wasn't trying to make him feel guilty, but her little gesture did exactly that. Who was he to promise that he wasn't going to do anything to hurt her? If any of the others on the quest had asked him, he would have said the same thing— and he hadn't come close to delivering on that promise.

"You seem like a nice man, Mr. Steadfast. Not everybody here is so nice."

"What do you mean? Has someone here done bad things to you?"

She shook her head quickly. "Not to me. To one another. I've been in a few of these rooms—I really like that one with all the computers and stuff down the hall—and sometimes people show up when I don't think they will. Like I said, I'm a good hider, so no one ever sees me. But I've heard people say really mean things to one another and sometimes they talk about taking things away from other people or telling them they're fired and can't work here anymore."

Steadfast tried to parse what the little girl was saying. As best he could tell, she'd overheard conversations about staff cuts and maybe some unpleasant bullying. At this point, none of it surprised him. There was a dark side to the Verity culture that had seeped in over the years.

"Have you heard a lot of these mean conversations?"

"Not a lot. There are a couple of men who are *really* mean, and they don't let other people talk."

Steadfast had an idea about who one of the mean guys might be. "We really need that treasure, don't we?"

"Treasure?"

Steadfast tried to explain the quest in an age-appropriate way, which was both easier and harder than he imagined it would be. He left out the scariest parts of the story, but he acknowledged that it was only his first day but he'd already let his people down, and now he'd abandoned them.

"Once, my mama said if I made a mistake, I should say I'm sorry to that person. And then I should say sorry to me, too."

Steadfast allowed himself a moment to absorb her wisdom. "Your mama gave you some very good advice, Dawn."

The little girl nodded solemnly. As Steadfast considered what she was saying, he noticed again the white rose on her headband. It reminded him of his wife's white rosebushes, which he had forgotten to water while she was away recently. He had apologized to her and promised to be more diligent in the future (which he had been), and she let him off the hook. Maybe if he did the same thing with his team, they could continue on together.

"Yes, you're right. Everyone makes mistakes and does some

things that don't work out as intended. I've had quite a bit of experience with that today. I need to apologize for that—and to apologize to myself as well."

Suddenly the cup on the conference room table started to glow. Dawn gasped. As they watched, the word FORGIVENESS shone inside the cup and joined the others as it was etched around the side. Steadfast couldn't avoid the obvious: He really needed to seek forgiveness from both his team and himself. He might not have lived up to his ideal of what it meant to be the CEO, but perhaps there was still hope.

"Was that magic?" the girl said.

"That does appear to be the only explanation."

She examined the cup closely. "What's this stuff inside?"

Steadfast expected the few drops of elixir that had been there earlier. Instead, he found the cup nearly half full. He'd been revived, along with the cup's contents.

"I'm still trying to figure that out, but it's speaking to me."

Dawn furrowed her eyebrows. "*The gold stuff* is speaking to you."

He smiled at her. "In its way. Come on, would you like to meet my friends?"

Her expression showed concern. "They're not going to turn me in, are they?"

"That's really not something you need to worry about right now. Will you join us?"

"Um, sure."

"I'm very glad to hear you say that."

Steadfast latched the cup to his belt again and then reached for Dawn's hand. She took it, and they headed down the hall.

CHAPTER 18

Trying Again

We need to use our talents in the best possible
way and concentrate our energies to avoid anything that might distract us from our goal. We
can't get sidetracked no matter who or what tries
to stop us.

—Steadfast

When Dawn and Steadfast got to the communications center,
the scene was very similar to the one Steadfast had left. Reposit
was still on the floor, though he appeared less dazed. Stout was
sitting next to him, running rudimentary tests to check his
responses. Whatever adversarial relationship they'd had at the
start of the day appeared to be gone as they laughed with each
other. Joe was starting to find places for all the things that had
been blown about. Considering how destructive the fan had
been, it was going to take quite some time.

Loop was ensconced in his laser beam web, typing furiously
on his phone. The beams were so tightly concentrated, Steadfast
couldn't read any of them. It was probably for the best. Meanwhile, Hoggit's interview was still playing on the screens in
repeat mode, which meant the COO would soon be announcing
again that Steadfast wasn't CEO material. Steadfast was simply
going to have to tune him out.

It took the others a moment to notice Steadfast had returned. When she saw him, the sergeant rose to her feet.

"Good to see you back, sir."

"It's good to be back, Ernesta."

He looked at Reposit. "How are you doing, professor?"

Reposit attempted a smile, though it was weak. "I'm going to be fine. The sergeant has been taking good care of me." He patted his satchel. "And this is all in one piece."

Joe stepped away from the computer bank and stood next to Stout. "We have a pretty big mess here."

Steadfast glanced around the room. "We're going to have to get a cleanup crew and a tech crew in here."

Steadfast gestured over to Loop, but the man was consumed in his updating.

"I owe you all an apology. I'm sorry I walked out on you. I was overwhelmed and feeling useless because I've led us from one threatening situation to another. I wasn't trusting you or being honest about my own doubts."

"No need to apologize, sir," Stout said.

Reposit pushed himself to his feet. He appeared a little unsteady, but it didn't seem like he was going to topple. "We appreciate it, and we accept your apology, but Ernesta's right. You've done as well as any leader could under these crazy circumstances."

Joe raised a hand. "I second that."

Steadfast was full of emotion. He'd hoped for forgiveness, but he was getting so much more. "Thank you all."

At that point, he remembered Dawn standing quietly next to him. Steadfast introduced her to the others, sharing a bit of her story. Dawn filled in a few more details, though she absolutely refused to explain how she avoided the security cameras every night.

"It sounds like you're a very bright girl," Reposit said. "And quite resourceful. That could prove extremely valuable as we continue on our quest."

As he said this, the professor glanced meaningfully at Steadfast.

"Yes, about that. Dawn has given me a little extra inspiration in that regard. I think we do indeed need to keep going. It's the right thing to do. And if you'll still have me as your leader, I'd like to lead us."

The three agreed readily. Steadfast didn't even bother to see if Loop was listening.

"Finding the treasure is obviously much harder than we ever imagined. We need to use our talents in the best possible way and concentrate our energies to avoid anything that might distract us from our goal. We can't get sidetracked no matter who or what tries to stop us."

At that moment, Steadfast's cup glowed again and the word FOCUS etched itself on the glass.

Dawn tapped him on the arm and pointed to the cup. "Make sure you don't spill."

Steadfast looked at the cup again and noticed it was nearly three-quarters full. He smiled at the little girl.

"You don't need to worry about that. There's only one way this liquid disappears, and I know exactly how to avoid that." Looking at the rest of the group, he said, "Is everyone with me?"

They responded so quickly with positive nods and yeses, Steadfast felt humbled. "Okay, let's go find that treasure."

"Find that treasure," Loop said from his web in a voice that sounded more automaton than human. Maybe the red lasers were surrounding him so tightly that they were constricting his airflow.

Steadfast called after him. "Loop, I think it's time to power down that phone. We don't need everyone to know exactly what we're doing."

This only seemed to motivate Loop to type even faster, which made the laser web grow thicker and tighter. His body puffed up and his glasses fused to his face, becoming red circles around his eyes. His dreadlocks started growing toward the floor.

Dawn screamed (which seemed to Steadfast like an appropriate response). Loop's transformation wasn't finished, though. As the dreadlocks touched down, they turned into eight hairy legs. Within seconds, there was nothing recognizable about the Miles Loop they knew.

Stout reached for her truncheon. "He's turned into a giant spider. We need to stop him."

"I have a better idea," Steadfast said, thinking about the need to stay focused and avoid the terrifying thing Loop had become. "Let's run!"

Joe grabbed Dawn's hand and rushed her out the door. Stout had raised her arm, ready for battle, but then she turned, took Reposit's arm, and led him away. Steadfast allowed himself one more look at what Loop had become. He'd always been uneasy around spiders. If this was an effort to highlight his greatest fears, the effort was at least partially effective. He needed to get out of there.

He slammed the door behind him—hopeful it would keep Loop inside—and ran to catch up with his team.

CHAPTER 19

Upward

If there's a sign, we need to follow it.

—Steadfast

Steadfast caught up with the group as they were making their way down an interior hall. They slowed as Steadfast approached, Dawn gesturing toward something Steadfast couldn't see from his current angle.

"It's through there," she said.

Steadfast moved a little closer and saw she was pointing at an air duct on the wall near the floor. "What is?"

Joe spoke up. "Dawn was just telling me that she's seen another cupola sign."

"In the air duct?"

Dawn scoffed. "Not *in* the air duct. *Through* the air duct. That's where my room is."

"Your room?"

"The place I go when I don't want anyone to find me. We just have to crawl through this tunnel."

Joe knelt by the duct. "I can't think of where this leads."

Dawn bent down next to him. "That's because it's secret. It's very dusty."

Reposit threw up his hands. "I'm not buying any of this. I would know if there were secret rooms in Verity Tower."

Stout laughed, "Are you still trying to convince us you know everything there is to know about this place?"

Reposit hesitated, and then his face relaxed as he grinned at the sergeant. "I suppose I need to revise my thinking, huh?"

"Now you're using that slightly dinged-up head of yours, professor," she replied. Then Stout added, "Maybe this is the place Tiffany was telling us about earlier."

Steadfast shrugged. "At this point, anything is possible."

Joe pulled the covering from the vent. "There are no screws on this thing."

"I took them off," Dawn said. "So I could get in fast."

"Smart kid."

Stout shined her flashlight inside. She turned back to Steadfast. "Pretty tight fit, sir, but we could get through."

"If Dawn says there's another sign up there, I think we need to follow it. It's not like we have any better clues." He turned to the little girl. "Dawn, do you want to lead the way?"

"Sure."

She climbed inside without hesitation. As she did, Steadfast noticed the pink soles of her shoes. The rubber formed a sunburst pattern.

Who, exactly, is this girl?

The others followed her into the duct, with Steadfast going last. It was definitely a tight fit. Still, Steadfast managed to pull the grate back on to cover the opening and hide their passage from Hoggit and Loop.

The duct twisted around and upward. Their progress was slow. Eventually, though, Steadfast heard a duct cover fall to the floor ahead of him and he followed the others out.

He wasn't expecting what he encountered. They had entered a grand, sloping hallway. The ceiling was vaulted in a series of arches, like the ribs of a fantastic beast. A rainbow of shining glass, reminiscent of the bridge the hummingbird had created, connected each arch.

"Wow, this is some place," Joe said, the admiration apparent in his voice. "It's so bright in here, though. Where's the light coming from? It's not natural and it's not electric."

Dawn looked up at him. "It's magic."

Joe smiled. "Yeah, I guess it is."

The little girl pointed to the hallway. "Come on, my room's this way."

Steadfast felt Dawn's excitement as she moved ahead of the group. She was right about lots of dust here; Steadfast noticed she was creating little sunburst impressions in the fine powder as she walked away. He knew it was important to keep up with the girl but he couldn't stop himself from looking around. The walls were lined with empty display cases. After they'd passed a few, the professor stopped and rubbed a dust-covered brass nameplate.

"'*Leda*, 1910, by Daryl Bennu,'" he said. He moved to the next. "'*Water Nymph* from the Mythology Series, 1887.'" And the next. "Hey, Joe, this one called *Blossom Vase* was made by someone in your family."

Joe stopped in his tracks, calling for Dawn to wait. Then he turned back to the case. "It's empty, huh?"

Reposit nodded solemnly. "I'm afraid so."

"Gee. I wonder what it looked like."

"Maybe someday we'll find out."

Joe seemed to reflect for a moment; then he lifted his chin and continued following Dawn.

At the end of the long, arched hallway, Dawn stopped them and extended her hand as though she were a presenter on a game show. "This is it."

They were standing in a small, snug space with one round leaded glass window on the far wall.

"That's my bed," she said, pointing to a cushion made of mail-bags. The sight of it tore at Steadfast's heart. Dawn deserved so much more. She didn't seem to see it that way, though. She seemed proud of the place, much like a recent college grad might feel about her first closet-sized studio apartment.

She knelt and moved one of the mailbags, exposing a Sign of the Shining Cupola, etched into the wall. It seemed to glow around the edges. "Here's that sign I was talking about. It's my night light."

Steadfast knelt next to her. "It's a beauty."

He pressed the sign, expecting something to happen, but nothing did. He pressed it again and still nothing. Stout and Joe did the same. Reposit didn't try, choosing instead to refer to *A Brief Compendium*.

"Maybe you need your cup," Dawn said to Steadfast.

Steadfast figured it was worth a shot. He unlatched the cup from his belt and touched it gently to the sign. Instantly, a quiet hum filled the air. A large section of the wall swung inward, revealing a winding stone stairway. Dawn squealed with surprise.

"The Arduous Stair," Reposit said, quickly flipping through his book.

Joe took one step toward the opening. "What's that?"

The professor found the page he was looking for and quickly showed it to the others before closing the book. "Only one of the most dangerous parts of the Worthy Way. According to my research, it's supposed to wind around the dome between the interior and exterior walls."

"That makes sense," Joe said. "They probably did it that way for maintenance."

The professor moved to the foot of the stairway. "Or to make it possible to reach the crystal cupola." He stepped forward but Steadfast stopped him.

"These stairs are very steep. We're going to need to be careful. Let me lead the way."

With that, they began yet another climb—on a day of constant spiraling, never moving in a straight line. Steadfast was glad he wasn't claustrophobic, because his shoulders were brushing the outer dome wall on one side and the inner dome wall on the other. A slight sense of panic began to rise in him as their destination seemed beyond reach.

Then, just as Steadfast was beginning to wonder if the climb would ever end, the stairs curved even more sharply—and he ran into a tangled mass of vines.

CHAPTER 20

Teardrops

> When you take care of the most magnificent things in your environment, they always reward you.
>
> —Steadfast

The thick vines were completely blocking the way. Steadfast was still breathing heavily from the tight, difficult climb and the thought of it leading to an impasse was beyond frustrating. Were they going to have to make their way back down this winding staircase, through Dawn's room, and then out the air duct? If so, what was their next move?

"Did we reach the top?" Stout called from a few steps below.

"No. Around the curve there are massive vines blocking us off."

The sergeant maneuvered herself past the others to stand next to Steadfast. "Wow, this thing is huge."

"Yes it is."

She bent toward the vine. "Kinda cool looking, though. The leaves have a pretty unusual shape, sort of like teardrops. And this might be the darkest green I've ever seen."

This seemed to catch the professor's attention, and he too squeezed his way up and stood next to Stout.

"Did you say dark teardrop leaves?" Reposit said. He examined the plant more closely. "I can't believe it. This is the extremely rare heartening plant. I've seen references to it in my research. It blooms only once every hundred years." He pointed into the vine. "Look, there's a bud."

Stout pulled a knife from her belt. "I'll just cut a way through this."

Reposit drew in a sharp breath. "Did you not hear what I just said? This is the rarest of plants. You can't just slash it to pieces."

"I can if we want to get where we're going."

Both of them turned to Steadfast. He stepped between them, even though there was little space, and he tried to gently pull the vine away from the wall. It didn't budge.

"Sir, would you mind if I gave it a try?" Stout said.

Steadfast inched aside and watched as the sergeant yanked at the vine with increasing force. The results were exactly the same. She brandished her knife again. "I think we're gonna have to start hacking."

Steadfast held up a hand to stop her. If Reposit was right about the rarity of the plant, cutting it to shreds seemed criminal. Still, if they didn't find a way to get past the vine, they would have to seek another route to the crystal cupola. There were two problems, though. None of them seemed to know any other routes. And they were on borrowed time. Hoggit had to be somewhere in the building, and he'd already made it clear he would do whatever he needed to do to complete his agenda.

If I turn back now, Steadfast thought, *the quest will almost certainly fail.* He hated the idea of destroying something precious, but he knew that a huge number of people were counting on him. Letting them down would be worse.

He reached his hand to Stout. "Let me have the knife. If someone is going to do this, it should be me."

The sergeant handed over the blade and then took a step down to give Steadfast more room.

The knife grip felt cold in his hand. For nearly a minute, he held it, motionless. He knew what he had to do; he just hated the idea of doing it. At last, he knelt by the vine and began to cut. As he did, he caught a glimpse of his cup. It was only a third full of elixir now, significantly less than the last time he looked. He thought again about the words etched onto the cup on this momentous day. The words celebrated virtues, which Steadfast strongly believed in. Was destroying something exceedingly rare a virtuous act, even when he needed to do it to help so many others?

He looked back at the plant. He could see the bud the professor had mentioned earlier, and on closer inspection he found numerous others. This vine was getting ready to blossom into something magnificent, even after a hundred years of dormancy, surviving in a place with very little light.

He put the knife on the step next to him. "No. This isn't the right thing to do. We can't destroy this extraordinary thing just to get what we want."

His cup started to glow. Steadfast looked to see a new word illuminating the glass: STEWARDSHIP. Was that what he was doing here? Was he being a steward to the plant's future? Did he understand the value the plant brought to the world, even if few would ever get to see it? Did it complicate things for him and his team? Regardless, the cup was filling once again.

Dawn edged up to him. "That is the craziest cup."

Before Steadfast even realized what she was doing, Dawn dipped her fingers into the elixir. Instinctively, he pulled back, startling Dawn. She flung her hand out and some of the drops of elixir landed on the vine.

What happened next was astounding, even measured against the events of this day. The dark leaves on the vine started to rustle, the buds began to swell, and flowers began to burst to life—white, heart-shaped flowers that carried with them the sweet scent of honey. And then the vine began to undulate. At first it simply seemed like a graceful dance. But then Steadfast noticed something else—the vine was retracting enough to leave him and his team room to slip through and continue up the tower.

"See?" Dawn said. "The plant is letting us go. You didn't have to cut it down after all."

Steadfast was amazed by the joy he felt in his heart. He had already known he'd done the right thing, but this latest display of magic was a gift he'd remember for the rest of his life. When you take care of the most magnificent things in your environment, they always reward you.

He bowed close to the still-waving plant. "Thank you," he said.

Then he turned to the others and waved them up, toward the crystal cupola.

※

CHAPTER 21

Taking Hold

There was no way he was going to fall with so
many people supporting him.

—Steadfast

The magical vines were awe-inspiring, but they could help only
so much. They were no match for the thick stone wall that they
encountered just twenty steps beyond the magical plant.

"We've arrived at a dead end," Stout said, exasperated. "After
all this?"

Reposit poked his head around the curve and gasped. "This
can't be. The Arduous Stair is supposed to lead to the crystal
cupola. I've found numerous references to this."

"Hang on a moment," Steadfast said, looking for bits of light.
He pointed to his left. "Look. There's light coming through some
sort of shaft. Maybe it's just big enough."

Stout craned her neck in that direction. "Big enough for
what, sir?"

"Big enough to crawl through."

Maintaining his focus, Steadfast did exactly that. He started
crawling ahead and shouted back to report what he saw. "There's
a circle of sky at the end."

Steadfast could hear the others behind him, and shortly they all reached the spot where he was now standing. They looked at him expectantly.

In that moment Steadfast was experiencing vertigo—as much from the view of the miniaturized activity on the city streets more than five hundred feet below as from the expectations of the people surrounding him. All day, he found himself leading with confidence one moment and then freezing up just as quickly when the next step wasn't clear. And he'd find himself immobilized as he faced the expectations of his team. He supposed his anxiety of heights was a metaphor for all the fears he needed to get over to be the effective leader he had always imagined himself becoming. Taking another deep breath, Steadfast looked around and saw he was surrounded by expanses of curving white marble. Just at the edge of his vision, he could see the tip of the crystal cupola overhead.

He turned back to the others. "We're in the dome. The cupola isn't far away."

"That's fantastic news," Reposit said.

"Well, it is and it isn't. We've come to the end of the tunnel. Joe, can you take a look outside?"

The window washer squeezed past a few of the others, opened one of the windows and leaned out, looking up toward the cupola.

"Do you think we could climb up the dome?" Steadfast asked.

Glancing in every direction, Joe took a long time to answer. "I don't see how we could do it. The marble is way too slick."

"I was afraid you were going to say that. What if we were all connected by that rope at your belt?"

"That would help, but we'd still need something to hold onto. Otherwise, it would be way too easy to slip and, I don't know if you noticed, but it's a long way down."

Steadfast shuddered involuntarily. "Oh, I noticed."

Just then, a clicking sound echoed behind them, coming from somewhere inside the inner dome walls.

"What was that?" Dawn said, sounding like a frightened little girl.

The clicking continued. Steadfast looked at Stout, who mouthed the word "spider" to him. The transformed Loop was after them.

Steadfast headed back toward the window. "I need to go farther out. Joe, can you hold onto my legs?"

"You got it."

"And I've got you," Stout said to Joe.

"And I you," the professor said to Stout.

"And I . . . well, you know," Dawn said, imitating the others.

This chain of support emboldened Steadfast. There was no way he was going to fall with so many people supporting him. He leaned out farther than Joe had, feeling a trickle of fear running up his spine and choosing to ignore it. *A spider in one direction and an enormous drop in the other,* he thought. *I guess I'm going to be facing my fears any way I turn.*

Once again, he saw the shining tip of the crystal cupola. They were so close to it now. He scanned the marble for anything to hang onto and found nothing. Or did he?

He watched in surprise as raised shapes began to appear on the face of the marble. One was only a few feet away—a handhold in the shape of the Sign of the Shining Cupola. He saw other handholds extending toward the top.

He pulled himself back inside and told the others what he'd seen.

"Handholds on the outside of the dome?" Reposit said.

Steadfast smiled at him. "I guess Verity Tower still has a lot of secrets to reveal to you, professor."

Reposit, at a loss, simply shook his head.

Meanwhile, Joe unhooked the rope from his belt and Steadfast watched as he methodically started making the first knot while he explained to the others how he would link them together.

Stout balked. "This sounds pretty dangerous."

Joe started to speak again when the clicking sounds—definitely closer now—echoed through the shaft.

Steadfast caught Stout glancing behind her and then back at Joe. "On the other hand, getting eaten by a giant spider sounds way more dangerous." Within a couple of minutes, Joe had roped everyone together. It was time to ascend the dome.

Joe must have seen Steadfast hesitating, because Joe leaned toward him and whispered. "I can go first, if you'd like. As you could probably guess, I don't have any trouble with heights."

Steadfast looked away from Joe and at the others. They were all watching him, obviously aware of what was going on, even though Joe had tried to be discreet. It wouldn't be the worst thing in the world to let the window washer go first. Leaders had to know when to delegate, right? Maybe he could even say he wanted to go last so he could have everyone's backs. That didn't feel right to Steadfast, though. He could see that it wasn't technical skill that he or anyone needed. It was a simple slope to climb. He had what it took—he just had to find it in himself. He had to face his fear. At the time of their greatest peril, he needed to take charge, even with all the worry and apprehension coursing through his veins.

"Thanks, Joe, but I've got it."

Joe's smile was illuminated by a glow from Steadfast's cup. A new word twinkled in the glass: COURAGE. Steadfast looked up from the cup to see a collection of smiling faces.

Then the clicking returned.

"I think it's time to get out of here," he said, pulling himself up through the opening.

CHAPTER 22

Not Quite Crystal Clear

Maybe he wanted to believe in a kind of company that didn't exist. Yet he still held on to the hope that there was something deeper and more lasting below the surface, and sticking together, they could get a glimpse of it.

—Steadfast

Steadfast knew he had to be strong for his team. It was all about staying focused on his destination, moving up one handhold at a time—and definitely not looking down, which also meant not looking back at the others. He would have to trust that as long as he felt the rope that linked them together, they were going to be okay.

Maybe fifteen minutes after they'd started, Steadfast felt the curve of the dome flattening. Lifting himself farther, he pulled up to stand on the narrow deck that encircled the outside of the crystal cupola. Now that he could turn to the others, he used the rope to help bring them onto the deck. Then he considered the structure in front of them. The cupola was divided into glass panels supported by a silver framework. It was shining in the afternoon sky. Peering through the dulled glass, he caught glimpses of a crystal reflecting every color of the rainbow, displaying spots of rose, yellow, and blue. From street level, the cupola was beautiful, but not particularly imposing. Standing next to it, though, was a different story. Steadfast was surprised by its scale: It had to be at least twenty-five feet tall.

Joe helped untie everyone. As soon as he was free, the professor moved as close as he could to the cupola. "The treasure! It's just inside. After all these years, I'm finally going to see it."

Steadfast could appreciate Reposit's excitement, because it mirrored his own, even if their reasons were likely somewhat different. Each team member leaned close to peer through the glass at the crystal. Steadfast took up a place between the professor and Dawn, cupping his hands around his eyes. He was hoping to see the Treasure Beyond All Price, but all he got was his own reflection.

"It's so bright I can't see in," Stout said.

Dawn pushed her nose directly up against the glass. "Me either."

Joe stepped back and moved right several panels. "We're getting too much glare from the sun. Visibility should be better on the east side."

As they all shifted, Dawn started counting the panels.

"Eleven," Joe said to her. When she looked at him curiously, he added, "I already counted."

Now standing next to Joe on the other side of the cupola, Steadfast tried gazing in again. The results were no better this time. He looked at the window washer.

"Are you seeing anything?"

"Nah, nothing."

Steadfast felt his spirits drop.

"I'm guessing the inside is too dingy. I'll bet nobody's washed it in a really long time."

Steadfast considered this an apt metaphor for the operations at Verity. Looking at Joe, he asked, "How do we get in? Is there an entrance from the inside?"

Joe didn't have an answer, so Steadfast queried the professor, who immediately took out his *Brief Compendium*. After a minute or so thumbing through the pages, he closed the book and shrugged. "I've got nothing."

Steadfast leaned against the cupola and looked out on the city. From below, this edifice was a symbol of everything that had gone right in Harken, a city that had persevered when so many others had stumbled. Now, looking down, he was beginning to wonder if the cupola was nothing more than a mirage, or, in his case, a false idol. Maybe he wanted to believe in a kind of company that didn't exist. Yet he still held on to the hope that there was something deeper and more lasting below the surface, and together they could get a glimpse of it. Maybe they had a bit of time left to figure it out.

He allowed himself this one moment of reflection and then lifted his head and turned to his team. "Okay, so climbing up here wasn't the answer. Let's go back down the dome and find a safe place to reassess."

The others seemed ready to follow when a dreaded sound reoccurred.

Click. Click. Click.

The spider was still on their trail. Steadfast looked over the edge of the landing and saw the huge arachnid beginning to skitter up the side of the dome without any need of handholds.

"Is that what I think it is?" Stout said.

"I'm afraid so. We need to get out of here now."

The professor's frightened voice cut through the air. "But where are we going to go? The spider is coming up from where we came, we're not tied together anymore, and—"

"Here," Joe said, pointing toward the east side of the dome. "There are more handholds going down the other side."

Steadfast knew there was no time to tie everyone together

again. "Joe, lead the way. I'll go last in case I need to fight off the spider."

Stout came up next to him. "That's my job, sir."

"No it's not, Ernesta. Not under these circumstances. Go join the others. But maybe you could leave me your truncheon."

The sergeant took the weapon from its holster and handed it to Steadfast. "Be safe, sir."

"Go."

Steadfast heard the others scrambling, with Joe shouting instructions and encouragement. As the spider that had once been Loop showed its first two hairy legs on the landing, the window washer called out, "Everybody's down, Steadfast."

Just before turning to join them, Steadfast saw the huge red-rimmed eyes of the spider peering at him. Steadfast ran toward the other side of the dome. He could hear the spider skittering behind him, snapping its jaws. In the distance, he heard Stout announce they'd found a hatch.

Paying no heed to his acrophobia—another fear on his long list—Steadfast found the first handhold with his feet and started lowering himself just as the spider reached the handholds, too. With its hairy legs only a few feet away, Steadfast was convinced he was about to become a midday snack. *Maintain your courage,* he thought. *Pretend it isn't there.*

And then Joe and the sergeant were pulling him through the hatch. The spider was about to join them, poking its head in the opening and gnashing its teeth. But quickly, Steadfast and Stout slammed the door shut and locked their tormentor outside. The spider might have been terrifying, but it couldn't reach them now.

CHAPTER 23

Finding Treasure

Always keep your cup full and your life will overflow with joy.

—Nora

The hatch had deposited them onto a balcony near the top of the dome. Steadfast could feel the adrenaline coursing through his system and his heart pumping fast as he sat on the floor and tried to catch his breath. After climbing up the tower, ascending the marble dome, then escaping a murderous spider, he had to admit he was exhausted, yet elated. He laughed at the craziness of it all.

When they heard him, the others, who all seemed to be in their own various stages of recovery, circled him, looking concerned.

He held up a hand. "I'm fine." He chuckled again. "It's been quite a day, hasn't it?"

They all nodded and looked around once again at their surroundings. From where Steadfast was sitting, he could look up at the bottom of the cupola, but from this perspective it appeared to be little more than a sooty cap on the dome. Faint streaks of light snuck through cracks in the grime.

Joe looked up as well. "I was right about the inside of that thing being blackened by years of neglect."

Steadfast nodded. "I still don't see how anyone in charge of a company this proud could have ever let that happen."

"Taking care of the legacy becomes less and less important over the years," Reposit said. "Until you get to the point where the legacy goes dark."

Dawn scooted next to him. "It still looks nice from the outside."

Steadfast smiled at her. "It does, Dawn. But that's not nearly good enough."

He turned to the others. "I don't think the treasure is in there."

Reposit bowed his head. "I don't get it. The clues suggested it—in so many different ways. How could they all have been wrong?"

The professor pulled out *A Brief Compendium* and began leafing through it. Watching him devotedly poring over his life's work, Steadfast felt a rush of affection toward the bookish man who'd dedicated so much to the history of Verity.

He looked at Stout, still standing at attention after everything they'd been through, still ready to cover his back.

He looked at Joe, who was probably right now trying to figure out how to get inside the cupola so he could bring it back to its gleaming heyday.

And then he looked at Dawn, who had already faced such major challenges in her life and still had the imagination and spirit to look at the bright side of things.

Over the course of the day, this group of disparate souls had learned to work as a team. Even when their lives were literally hanging in the balance, they'd stuck together.

Suddenly, Steadfast heard a sound like fluttering to his left. He turned to look, finding the glass hummingbird that had been so helpful to them earlier hovering nearby. With it were all of the sculptures from the garden that had escaped the factory fire, along with others he hadn't seen before, all animated. And with them, grinning her elfin grin, was Tiffany. Steadfast was full of emotion. *Maybe she found the storeroom. Maybe we are just at the beginning of the real adventure.*

"Did we miss anything?" she said.

The group laughed. Stout walked over to give Tiffany a hug and introduce her to the newest members of the group. Steadfast marveled at the sight.

"I just need to say something," Steadfast said, after the introductions had been made. "Our quest might not be turning out the way we thought, but you guys mean more to me than I could ever say."

They all looked at him and Steadfast felt a connection unlike any he'd experienced before. He realized he'd been searching for this type of connection with colleagues his entire career, one that even transcended the relationship he had with Nora. Steadfast felt the emotion thrumming through him—until he realized it wasn't emotion, but the cup at his belt shining to life again. He unhooked it and saw the new word that had emblazoned itself among all the others: CONNECTION. He held the cup up to the group, showing them the inscription. As he did, he noticed the glowing elixir inside was nearly to the brim.

"I can't read all of these words," Dawn said.

Steadfast held the cup out to her. "I can help with that. We have RESPONSIBILITY, CURIOSITY, COOPERATION, TRUST, TRUTH, HOPE, FORGIVENESS, FOCUS, STEWARDSHIP, COURAGE, and now this new one, CONNECTION."

"These are good things, huh?"

"Yes. Very good things."

"Aw, what a precious scene." The voice came from just down the hall. Steadfast stood and turned. What he saw was an imposing beast, half man, half boar. Hoggit. Or at least what was left of him, with the spider just behind him.

The COO nodded snidely at Steadfast, then threw his head back and laughed. As he did, his pink tie—more like a huge pink tongue at this point—reached across the distance and snatched a couple of the animated glass sculptures. Hoggit popped each into his mouth as Steadfast had seen him do with the candies earlier. Then he laughed boisterously again.

Tiffany and Reposit moved to stand in front of the sculptures, with the hummingbird bobbing its head above them. Steadfast watched for a moment before turning his attention back to the rogue COO.

"Hoggit, I thought I fired you earlier and ordered you to leave the building."

The boar-man-beast stepped forward, growling, while Steadfast held his ground. "You know what, Steadfast? You have a great sense of humor—not to mention a hilarious imagination. Did you find the treasure, or do I have to do *everything* around here myself?"

Before he could answer, Steadfast felt the cup thrumming. He'd momentarily forgotten he was even holding it. He stole a quick glance to see the elixir inside bubbling rapidly, as though it were coming to a boil.

When he looked back at Hoggit, Steadfast saw that the COO's eyes had fixed on the cup. Reflexively, Steadfast drew it closer to himself.

"That cup!" Hoggit said. "There's something about it. I must have it. Give it to me."

Dawn yelled at him. "Don't do it, Mr. Steadfast. That's your precious thing."

The cup was boiling more furiously now, with golden bubbles

rising toward the cupola. *That's your precious thing.* Dawn was right. The gift his mentor had bestowed upon him, a creation from Verity's greatest days, *was* precious to him.

Always keep your cup full and your life will overflow with joy.

It was his treasure.

His *Treasure*.

As soon as this thought formed in his mind, the golden bubbles seemed to form the word STEADFAST in the air.

Hoggit's voice bellowed. *"GIVE IT TO ME!"*

Steadfast had no interest in doing the madman's bidding and he was no longer afraid of any spider. Instead, he brought the cup to his lips and drank the golden elixir. It tasted of dreams, and promise, and visions fulfilled. It refreshed him as no drink had done before, making him feel stronger than he realized. He drank his fill, but when he finished, the elixir was still bubbling near the top of the cup.

Each of the eleven virtues shimmered and warmed his hands:

RESPONSIBILITY
CURIOSITY
COOPERATION
TRUST
TRUTH
HOPE
FORGIVENESS
FOCUS
STEWARDSHIP
COURAGE
CONNECTION

The glow grew hotter and more intense, shifting from silver to cobalt blue and streaming toward the cupola. The light coalesced around the blackened glass, sparking and pulsing—until, in a flash, it dissipated, leaving behind a cupola so sparkling clean that Steadfast could see the words on his cup had now etched themselves in scrolling script on each of the glass panels of the cupola.

Sunlight was now pouring through the glass panels, bathing Verity Tower in a brilliance Steadfast knew had been missing for a very long time. He saw the others looking up in awe.

That's when he remembered Hoggit. Hoggit wouldn't find this wonder mesmerizing. He would find it threatening. He had to be stopped.

Steadfast pivoted, ready to do battle, but what he saw stunned him. Hoggit was folding in on himself as he attempted to shield his eyes from the light. His tusks were shrinking, his huge belly disappearing, and his tail was curling inward. Within a minute, he lay on the floor, disheveled, vaguely resembling the man Steadfast had met during his interviews—though Steadfast would never again be able to see Hoggit the same way.

Next to him lay Loop, in human form, finally speechless, with his red glasses cockeyed on his face and their lenses missing.

While the others were still gaping at the cupola, Steadfast walked to Hoggit and stood over him.

"I'll have Ernesta escort you out of the building, and, Ernesta, take Loop with you while you're at it."

Hoggit sneered but said nothing, all of his bluster gone. He'd made his power play and come up wanting. There was no "treasure" of the kind he sought. The treasure was in the people, their shared purpose and integrity. There was no way Hoggit would ever have come out on top, no matter how many acolytes he collected.

Just then, Steadfast heard Dawn's voice. "Oh, my."

He went over to her to see what she was reacting to. Maybe it was the dazzling light coming from the cupola and bathing the entirety of Verity Tower, making it seem as new as the day it opened. More likely, though, it was the radiant glass bridge, alive with every color of the rainbow, arcing from one side of the dome to the other. As it formed, the sculptures flew up to hover around it. Even the drawings Tiffany had brought back with her in Reposit's tubes popped out, unfurled, and ascended to the bridge.

The top of the bridge curved inside the base of the crystal cupola. There, surrounded by the shining virtues, stood a woman holding a goblet.

It was the elevator operator. Only now she was wearing the pale blue beaded gown he'd seen in a portrait in the gallery.

"The founder," he said softly. "Crystal Modello."

The woman smiled and raised her goblet toward Steadfast, just as Dawn ran over to her and wrapped her arms around her legs. Steadfast smiled at the sight and raised his cup—no longer bubbling, but still filled—in salute. Just then, he heard a great whooshing sound and he turned back toward the balcony. The pink slips that had covered the lobby floor were streaming up, where they vanished in a series of starbursts upon contact with the cupola.

When the ascension of paper finally subsided—and it took some time—Crystal Modello and Dawn were gone, with a starburst trail hanging in the air. Steadfast didn't dare try to make sense of it, but deep inside he knew everything was all right. He looked at the others and caught their eyes; they all smiled together.

The bridge to the cupola remained, though, as did the virtues etched in each of its glass panels. Slowly, the sculptures and the drawings floated back down to Steadfast and his companions, returning to their original state.

Tiffany picked up a delicate, multicolored orchid sculpture. "We need to figure out something to do with all of these." She gestured to the drawings. "And we definitely need to figure out something to do with all of those. They're too precious to be in danger ever again."

Steadfast smiled at her. "Sounds like our head designer is going to be very busy."

Her expression was wistful. "I might need a few additions to staff."

"I'm going to have to take a good look at our finances, but consider it one of my top priorities."

Reposit picked up the drawings and started rolling them back into the tubes. "I'll definitely need to add another chapter to *A Brief Compendium*."

"That you will," Steadfast said. "I don't think you should worry about keeping your compendium brief, though, professor. We have many new chapters to write."

They certainly did. Verity had suffered some serious damage today, especially to the factory, which was their lifeblood. And who knew how much damage Hoggit had caused during his insane power play. It was going to take a lot of effort to put everything back together and to bring Verity to its future glory. But Steadfast knew beyond a doubt that Verity had a great team and there would be many people dedicated to Verity's cause. He looked forward to serving them all.

He took one more look up at the cupola, at the virtues displayed on the panels and at the bridge where he'd seen the founder standing just a short while before. He tipped his cup in that direction one more time.

"I promise to serve you well. Our work has just begun."

CHAPTER 24

∽

A Celebration

I hope you will fill your cup with good things and I hope you'll always remember that by giving more to others than you take, your cup will always be full.

—Steadfast

As Steadfast walked into the atrium, he could feel his energy rising. He couldn't believe his luck. After days of rain, the sun was shining through the huge glass entry and the entire lobby was filled with late-afternoon light. He could practically feel the warmth on his skin, but he had a hunch the feeling was coming from deep inside.

In the center of the broad, circular space, nestled on a simple glass stand, sat the unassuming glass cup. It was the gift Nora had given him when he took the new job. For Steadfast, it symbolized Nora's faith in him and, in turn, the faith he knew he could place in Verity's employees. But he realized right away that this treasure was something he wanted to share with everyone, and not just keep for himself.

In fact, the handcrafted display was the first and only redecorating of the building he had ordered since his arrival. It was a daily reminder that what they most needed to succeed was more of what Verity already had: its core values, the values that went into each and every product they produced.

He slowly turned to take everything in. He saw the founders' balcony and the polished marble floor. He eyed the special Verity symbols he could see tucked here and there, on door handles, the banister, and elevator buttons. Sometimes he wondered if other people noticed them. They always made him smile. Everywhere he looked, there were unspoken reminders of the founder, all the predecessors who kept Verity going and growing, and whose contributions were recorded in the company history book and captured in the beauty of the glassware.

Looking back at the cup, he sensed there would always be a mystery around it, and Nora might never fully explain how she came to have it. But he had to wonder. Did she know about its magic? Did she experience it, too? Did she receive it as a gift from a mentor of her own—maybe someone he'd never heard her talk about? The questions tumbled through his mind, but one last one lingered in his thoughts. Would the cup always reside at Verity as a reminder of the belief we have to have in one another, or would he one day pass on the gift to someone else?

But there was no more time for reflection. It was time to greet and mingle with his colleagues as they waited for the official start of the event.

"Ahem, ahem. Shhhh...Shhhh...Hello, everyone. Hello. Welcome. I'm Nora Northstar."

When had Nora slipped in, without even coming over to say hello?

"I'm so thrilled to be here with you today as the honorary chair of the Association of Business and Community Leaders of Harken. As I'm sure you've all heard, Verity Glassworks had the distinguished honor of being chosen as Harken's Outstanding Company of the Year at last week's ceremony. Your CEO, Vince Steadfast, was there to accept the award. However, I don't think this part will surprise you: He couldn't formally accept it. He believes—and I concur—that this is a recognition for all of you in the room and so I am here to present the award to you this evening.

"What you all have done this year is remarkable. You took a company that was struggling during difficult times and you found your way back to your core values and purpose. You found your heart and your commitment to one another. You took what was already fine glassware and you produced it with greater crafts-manship, efficiency, and, I might add, love. At the same time you made a commitment to the artistry and innovation that was in your founding DNA. The community of Harken is proud of you and indebted for all you bring to our city.

"Congratulations, and please give yourselves a round of applause.

"And now, a man who needs no introduction, a man full of passion, persistence, and humility, your CEO, Vince Steadfast."

"Hi, good evening. Greetings, everyone. As you can see, I can't stop smiling. While we can't rest on our past accomplish-ments and we have to keep doing what we're all doing, we can take a moment to pause and soak in this hugely deserved honor while we gratefully acknowledge one another and what we've achieved. Each of us has played a unique role in rebuilding Verity and becoming Harken's Outstanding Company of the Year. We found our core values—and we're living and working by them. You are all the greatest.

"During this past year, I think the most important thing we did is learn to believe in one another and ourselves. We found our way connecting to something bigger than our day-to-day work. We were fortunate to have the founder of Verity, the values she instilled, and this very building to guide us. We polished our surroundings in the same way people polish silver—or glassware—and it gave us hope and inspiration. Together we found ways to use our imaginations and to dream.

"On that note I want to propose a toast to all of us—as trays of specially made glass cups are passed around for a champagne toast. They are miniatures of the cup on display in this atrium, which reminds us every day of the values we need to live by: RESPONSIBILITY; CURIOSITY; COOPERATION; TRUST; TRUTH; HOPE; FORGIVENESS; FOCUS; STEWARDSHIP; COURAGE; CONNECTION.

"These special glass cups are Verity's gift to you and my thank-you for coming together to make such great things happen. My hope is that all of you continue to live your lives according to the values we've discovered together. I hope you will fill your cup with good things and I hope you'll always remember that by giving more to others than you take, your cup will always be full.

"To all of you."

"To all of us."

"To Nora."

"To the founders."

"Hear, hear."

"Now enjoy the food, music, and let's party."

Afterword

Looking back on my life in the corporate world, I realize it's not what position I held, what salary I earned, or which promotion I received that led to a full and satisfying life. What mattered was my cup. Was my cup filled to the brim as I lived and worked with good values? Or did it drain when I didn't act the way I knew was right?

And what really filled my cup? A new car, a bigger house, a promotion, an exotic vacation? No! Possessions never filled my cup. Not one drop. Material things don't affect the fullness of my cup. The level stayed the same no matter what I acquired. But, when I based my actions on good values, like truth, love, and cooperation, then my cup filled—my cup even grew! My life filled with satisfaction and happiness.

Tough situations came along, when it was hard to hold on to my convictions and do the right thing. When I acted on poor values—in selfishness, suspicion, or fear—my cup always drained. It shrank. When that happened, I had no sense of purpose or joy in my work or life.

Sometimes when my cup was empty, I wouldn't stop to wonder how it got that way. I'd simply get more angry and bitter, hurting everyone and everything around me. Sooner or later, I'd come to my senses and remember that even when everything around me is wrong, there's always a right thing to do. As soon as I changed what I was putting into my cup, I felt refreshed with purpose, joy, and peace of mind. The fullness of my cup came to be my guide.

How full is your cup?

Is your cup small and empty? Are you miserable? Do you think you're miserable because you don't have everything you want? Do you have everything you want and still feel unhappy? Or is your cup big and full? Are you happy and content no matter what? Do you bring the very best values to your life and workplace and then act on them, no matter the cost?

And of course, the fullness of your cup ripples far beyond your personal life. Steadfast found that the amount of golden elixir in his cup didn't affect only him, but everything around him. The fullness of your cup affects your family, your workplace, your community, and the world at large. An empty cup casts a shadow over everyone. A full cup shines for the good of many.

I hope Steadfast's story inspires you to fill your cup, keep it full, and make it grow. Happiness and satisfaction don't come from material gain or success in the workplace. Acting on good values is the key to personal fulfillment, and it's the power that can change the world—one golden drop, one cup at a time.

Acknowledgments

"Alone we can do so little. Together we can do so much."

There is nothing truer than this quote from Helen Keller. The fact is that we need one another. None of us really ever accomplishes anything on our own. Our families, our teachers, our coworkers, our friends, and even people we will never know all play a role in our lives and add value to our journey.

The same is true for *The Magic Cup*. Without the wonderful team of caring people who believed in its message and mission, it would still be an idea sitting in the back of my head.

I would like to personally thank all who gave of their time, energy, intellect, and creativity to bring it to life.

Lori Ann Grover, Dia Calhoun, Lou Aronica, and Janet Goldstein, thank you for being tireless and staying with this to the end.

Sydney Armstrong, Deidra Wager, Mike Schiller, Chip Adams, and Barry Franklin for your honesty and for continually pushing me to make it better.

Jonathan Lyons, my agent from Curtis Brown, for his total belief in the idea and for not letting me give up.

Kate Hartson, Alexa Smail, Melanie Gold, Andrea Glickson, and Katie Broaddus, the team at Hachette Book Group/Center Street, for believing in the story and the virtues, and for taking the risk in bringing it to market.

Becky Nesbitt for her editing with heart and soul.
Jeff Brotman, for his mentoring, teaching and friendship.
Kathy Lewis, without whom my life would come to a standstill.
Thanks to you all . . . for making my dream your dream.

Howard

Reading Group Guide

Applying the Lessons:
The Eleven Virtues of the Magic Cup

Responsibility. *Self-awareness. Engagement. Pro-action. Fortitude.* (page 20)

When Steadfast tells the elevator operator he will do all he can to help Verity Glassworks, the word RESPONSIBILITY is magically engraved on his cup. Do you act with strength and energy for the good of the team and the organization?

Curiosity. *Open-mindedness. Questioning. Fascination. Interest.* (page 29)

Steadfast hears about the notion of a quest and is simultaneously mystified and open-minded. Have you found that when you entertain seemingly crazy ideas and listen to unlikely people, new possibilities open up to you?

Cooperation. *Collaboration. Partnership. Connection. Communication.* (page 51)

When Steadfast urges Professor Reposit and Sergeant Stout to work as a team to escape the fire in the vault, a passage appears. Can you pinpoint times when acting cooperatively helped you be more effective? Are you supporting others through acts of cooperation?

Trust. *Confidence. Credence. Faith. Letting go.* (page 62)

Steadfast trusted the ribbon of glass would safely support him across the molten glass on the factory floor. Are you able to trust those around you? Are you trustworthy yourself? How does this benefit you and those around you?

Truth. *Factualness. Verity. Authenticity. Honesty.* (page 78)

When Steadfast stands in doubt on the window-washing scaffold, trying to balance the safe approach with the danger of the quest, he decides to continue when he realizes the pursuit of truth is worth the risks. How do you balance risks and rewards? How does your team keep you honest with yourself and with others?

Hope. *Inspiration. Promise. Aspiration. Belief.* (page 87)

At the midpoint of the arduous climb to the top of the tower, Professor Reposit hits a wall of fatigue. Steadfast helps him imagine a better future at Verity and gives him the hope he needs to go on. Does affirming a value ever help you move beyond an impasse?

Forgiveness. *Reprieve. Clemency. Leniency. Humility.* (page 98)

By following Dawn's advice to forgive himself for losing hope and abandoning his team, Steadfast is able to ask his team for forgiveness and continue the quest. Do you need to forgive another, or yourself, to move forward?

Focus. *Concentration. Aim. Direction. Persistence.* (page 101)

Steadfast loses focus and commitment when confronted with Hoggit's criticism of his leadership abilities during the TV interview. Are you focused in your current work, or have you allowed yourself to become distracted by competing demands, competing versions of the truth, or distracting opinions about what others think of you?

Stewardship. *Caring. Caretaking. Honoring. Respecting.* (page 110)

When Steadfast refuses to cut down the rare heartening plant, with its hundred-year flowering teardrop vines, he's respecting the values of beauty and nature and how they benefit the world. Do you steward the environment you live and work in?

Courage. *Bravery. Heroism. Fortitude. Intrepidness.* (page 115)

By realizing that letting people down would be worse than his falling off the dome, Steadfast finds the courage to overcome his fear of heights. Do you know your fears? How do you overcome them?

Connection. *Affection. Devotion. Loyalty. Love.* (page 122)

Steadfast's love for his team and their love for him is what leads them all to press on and find the Treasure Beyond All Price. Do you exhibit affection and loyalty in your words and actions?

Questions for Discussion
to Explore on Your Journey

1. Which part of Steadfast's story made you think of your own journey? Where are you most excited, stuck, or afraid?

2. Have you, like Nora Northstar, encouraged someone to move to another role or job for his or her own growth, despite it being a loss to you?

3. In a crisis, how do you manage to stay on the Worthy Way?

4. Have you stepped off the Worthy Way, perhaps looking for the Easy Way? (We all do at some point.) Has it worked out? When has it not? If not, how did you step back on?

5. How do you cope when things at work seem crazy and out of control? Do you give up and wait for other people to take over? Do you thrive on drama and even add to it? Do you take it upon yourself to fix it—relying on your team or going solo?

6. When have you felt most like a "we" at work? Do you feel that way now? Are there people in your organization or group who don't?

7. Do you take the time to appreciate and honor the skills of those who have made your organization?

8. It can be hard to discern the difference between illusion and reality in many organizations. Have you ever been in a situation in which your company was projecting one thing to the public when the truth was much worse? How did things turn out?

9. Do you have an art or way of working that you believe in, that is most true to you? How can you utilize it more fully?

10. Do you take the time to appreciate and honor the skills that have made your organization successful? What about the

people at all levels who do the work, make the things you produce, keep everything and everyone humming day to day? Do you honor them?

11. When has your cup been most full? When has it been least full? What impact did that have on your life, loved ones, business, and community?

12. What is the origin of your values? Have you identified them explicitly? How do you act on them?

13. In all your life experiences, both personal and professional, has one value proven to be the most important to you—and why?

14. If Steadfast had failed to save Verity Glassworks, would that mean it had been an error to take the position as CEO in the first place?

15. If failure was imminent, should Steadfast have been willing to compromise his values to achieve success for Verity Glassworks?

16. If Steadfast had failed to save Verity Glassworks, do you believe his value system would have been, or should have been, considered a failure as well? By himself or others?

17. Do you believe there is some magic that gives your company or department some special power, purpose, or value? Are there roots you need to get back to, find, develop, and share?

18. How full is your cup right now?

19. Where do you think Nora got the cup? Has anyone given you a gift that has had meaning beyond its value? Have you given such a gift to someone else?

About the Author

Photo credit: Lisi Wolf Photography

HOWARD BEHAR is a renowned business leader, author, speaker, and mentor. He served at Starbucks for a combined twenty-one years as both an officer and a board member. He was the president of North America and the founding president of Starbucks International. He lives in Seattle, Washington, with his wife, Lynn, where he is able to spend time with his children and grandchildren.